Contract Bridge
CARD-PLAY TECHNIQUE

# Contract Bridge
# CARD-PLAY TECHNIQUE

Norman Squire

PITMAN PUBLISHING

*First Published* 1976

PITMAN
Pitman House, 39 Parker Street, London WC2B 5PB

PITMAN MEDICAL PUBLISHING CO LTD
42 Camden Road, Tunbridge Wells, Kent TN1 2QD

FOCAL PRESS LTD
31 Fitzroy Square, London W1P 6BH

PITMAN PUBLISHING CORPORATION
6 East 43 Street, New York, NY 10017

FEARON PUBLISHERS INC
6 Davis Drive, Belmont, California 94002

PITMAN PUBLISHING PTY LTD
Pitman House, 158 Bouverie Street, Carlton, Victoria 3053

PITMAN PUBLISHING
COPP CLARK PUBLISHING
517 Wellington Street West, Toronto M5V 1G1

SIR ISAAC PITMAN AND SONS LTD
Banda Street, PO Box 46038, Nairobi, Kenya

PITMAN PUBLISHING CO SA PTY LTD
Craighall Mews, Jan Smuts Avenue, Craighall Park,
Johannesburg 2001, South Africa

© Norman Squire 1976
ISBN 0 273 00206 6

This book is sold subject to the Standard Conditions of Sale
of Net Books and may not be resold in UK below the net price
Text set in 11/12 pt. Monotype Baskerville at Western Printing Services.
Printed by photolithography and bound in Great Britain
at The Pitman Press, Bath

G.20:14

# Contents

# Preface

This is a book for the player who has played the game but who wishes to be able to play well, to know how to assess a hand and to be able to approach difficult hands with the proper technique. All the standard, correct plays are here, all in fact that the expert needs to know. Tables provide quick and easy reference; difficult plays are set out clearly and fully analysed.

The Sherlock Holmes section (Chapter 10), illustrating how the expert player thinks, is something fresh and should prove of great interest and attraction. The matrices of all squeeze plays are presented more completely than is usual in books on play. The rapport between partner is stressed and alternative methods of signalling offered. Many of the example hands are taken from world-class events and we see not only how tricky contracts should be handled but also the mistakes which are made by even the best players, why they make them and how to avoid them.

# Basic Play at No-trumps

The normal drill for defenders is to lead the suit in which they hope to establish winners by virtue of length before their side entries are removed. The declarer acts similarly, not cashing tricks simply because they are there, for they can be cashed at any time, but playing the suits in which he hopes to establish extra tricks.

The declarer's paramount task is to make his contract and when his established tricks are sufficient to achieve this he should normally cash them at once. Overtricks may be thought about when the contract is assured. True, they are worth 20 or 30 points a time but several may be made without affecting the score at all. 760 points is counted as 800 but so is 850; to move from 760 to 850 might take no less than four overtricks. If a risk has been taken to obtain even one of them the cost of failure would be anything from 350 to 900. Clearly therefore that game is not worth the proverbial candle.

## 3 NT in its simplest form

```
      ♠ A 4          N         ♠ K 8 6
      ♡ Q J 6 2                ♡ K 10 3
      ◇ K 3     W        E     ◇ A Q J 2
      ♣ K 9 5 3 2       S      ♣ J 10 4
```

*Contract*
3 NT by West
Lead: ♠ 3

West wins Trick 1 and immediately plays Hearts, continuing the suit until the ace is taken. The defence clears the Spade suit but West has established his nine tricks, two Spades, three Hearts and four Diamonds. A trick in Clubs might be made but the timing does no permit West even to try to make one. He cashes his nine tricks and then plays a Club. The ace is taken and winning Spades take the remaining tricks. Had West played a Club before cashing his tricks he would have gone down, losing three Spades and two aces.

## Moving on

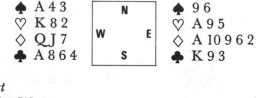

♠ A 4 3   ♠ 9 6
♡ K 8 2   ♡ A 9 5
◇ Q J 7   ◇ A 10 9 6 2
♣ A 8 6 4   ♣ K 9 3

*Contract*
3 NT by West
Lead: ♠ 5

An elementary play to sever the defenders' communications. West refuses to win with the Spade ace until the third round. Only then does he take the finesse in Diamonds. If South has the king he may not have another Spade to lead. If he has, the suit will have been divided four-four between the defenders and they take only three tricks in the suit plus their ◇ K. West makes the remaining nine. If West had taken his ace earlier and North had held a five-card suit, South would have won with his ◇ K and would still have had a Spade to lead. The contract would have failed, the defence taking one Diamond and four Spades.

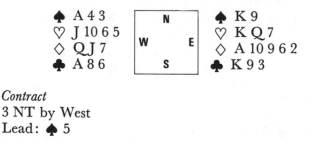

♠ A 4 3   ♠ K 9
♡ J 10 6 5   ♡ K Q 7
◇ Q J 7   ◇ A 10 9 6 2
♣ A 8 6   ♣ K 9 3

*Contract*
3 NT by West
Lead: ♠ 5

Now the first trick may be taken but the ♡ A must be knocked out before the finesse in Diamonds is taken. Should we take the finesse first, the Spades could be cleared for North while he still held a certain entry with the ♡ A. So Hearts are played, the ace taken and a Spade returned. This, as in the previous hand, is allowed to win, taking our second trick in the suit on the third round in order to sever communications again. And this means that Trick 1 must be taken by the ♠ K in dummy, not the ♠ A, for only by taking it with the king are we able to hold off the second round of the suit. If Spades break four-four the defence can take two Spades, one Diamond and one Heart, at most. If South had only three of the suit, West makes an overtrick.

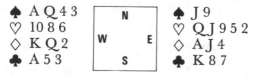

♠ A Q 4 3     ♠ J 9
♡ 10 8 6     ♡ Q J 9 5 2
◇ K Q 2     ◇ A J 4
♣ A 5 3     ♣ K 8 7

*Contract*
3 NT by West
Lead: ♣ 4

The contract cannot be made without establishing Hearts, but this requires that both tops held by the defence be removed. The first round of Clubs must therefore be ducked. The defence will assuredly make certain that the first round of Hearts is not taken by the hand which holds length in Clubs; they will preserve the entry in the same hand as the length. Consequently we duck the first round, not the second because when the first round of Hearts is taken we wish to have already severed the communication in Clubs. To take the first Club but duck the second is useless for North would simply overtake the lead and play a third round.

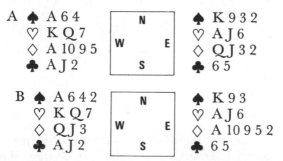

A   ♠ A 6 4     ♠ K 9 3 2
    ♡ K Q 7     ♡ A J 6
    ◇ A 10 9 5     ◇ Q J 3 2
    ♣ A J 2     ♣ 6 5

B   ♠ A 6 4 2     ♠ K 9 3
    ♡ K Q 7     ♡ A J 6
    ◇ Q J 3     ◇ A 10 9 5 2
    ♣ A J 2     ♣ 6 5

3 NT each time by West, the lead a small Club. With Hand "A" West overtakes South's queen with his ace, enters dummy with

a Heart and takes the Diamond finesse. He does not mind if it loses as North cannot play a further Club without conceding another trick in the suit. With Hand "B", however, the Diamond finesse is towards South. If it is wrong and West has taken the first Club he will be left in an untenable position, the lead going through his knave and another. With this hand therefore Clubs must be ducked twice. The play would be easier were that Club knave a small one. With the Diamond finesse wrong the stopping power of that knave is an optical illusion.

## Interlude for early test

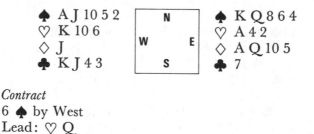

|  ♠ 6 3 | | ♠ A K 7 2 |
| ♡ 7 4 | | ♡ A K 8 3 |
| ◇ Q J 10 3 | | ◇ 9 5 |
| ♣ K 10 9 4 3 | | ♣ Q J 5 |

*Contract*
1 NT by West
Lead: ♠ Q

The first trick is taken in dummy. Please decide what to play at Trick 2.

The following hand is no certainty to make but there is a line of play which should succeed almost every time; nothing brilliant or unorthodox; just careful technique. Please decide your line of play.

| ♠ A J 10 5 2 | | ♠ K Q 8 6 4 |
| ♡ K 10 6 | | ♡ A 4 2 |
| ◇ J | | ◇ A Q 10 5 |
| ♣ K J 4 3 | | ♣ 7 |

*Contract*
6 ♠ by West
Lead: ♡ Q

Reverting to the first hand, this is sudden death; if you played anything except a Diamond at Trick 2 you went down. The Diamond is taken and the second Spade knocked out. We play another Diamond. The defence win this, cash two Spades (or

three Spades) and play a Heart. We take this, knock out the ace
of Clubs and have enough tricks to make our contract when the
second Heart comes.

If a Club is played at Trick 2 the defence duck two rounds,
take the third, cash two top Diamonds and end-play dummy
holding us to two tricks in each suit except Diamonds where we
make none. Even a switch to a Diamond after one Club is
ducked does not help; the defence simply duck a second Club
themselves and can still end-play the dummy.

The second hand is an example of giving ourselves every
possible chance to make a contract which cannot be absolutely
ensured.

Our object now is to create a position where his lead may be
profitable. The first trick should be taken in dummy, leaving us
with the king ten, safe from a lead by North, a finesse position if
the lead was irregular. Trumps are drawn in two rounds, ending
with West and the Diamond knave is played, because people
have been known to cover such a card. In fact if North has
K 9 8 6 he is very likely to do so. But we must assume that he
does not. We play the ace and then, and not before, play the
single Club from dummy. If South plays the Club ace when we
play the suit from dummy the hand is over so we must assume
that he does not. As he is likely to do so if he has it, we finesse
the knave and again must assume that it is won by North's
queen. Now if North leads either red suit he will establish our
twelfth trick for us while, should he return a Club, we have the
chance that the Club ace will drop on the third round of the
suit, failing which, the lead in dummy, we may either play
South for the Diamond king or play for it to drop in three. By
now of course we should have a good idea of the actual distribution, and this may have turned a possibility into a certainty.

|              | N          |              |
|--------------|------------|--------------|
| ♠ K Q 10     |            | ♠ J 6 4 2    |
| ♡ K J 2      | W        E | ♡ Q 7        |
| ◇ A K 10 6   |            | ◇ J 9 3      |
| ♣ A 8 6      | S          | ♣ J 9 5 2    |

*Contract*
3 NT by West
Lead: ♡ 3

The lead suggests that Hearts are breaking four-four, which is fortunate. West's knave wins Trick 1 and he attacks Spades but the defence holds off until the third round, so isolating dummy's knave, and then play ace and another Heart. As that ♠ J is the ninth trick dummy needs an entry. West therefore plays the ◇ 10 and puts the knave on it. This must be taken, and now dummy's nine provides the necessary entry.

## Establishment, safety and ethics

|  |  |  |
|---|---|---|
| ♠ Q J 10 | N | ♠ A K 9 |
| ♡ A J 7 |   | ♡ 8 6 |
| ◇ A Q 6 4 3 | W    E | ◇ K 5 2 |
| ♣ 7 5 | S | ♣ A 10 8 4 2 |

| *Contract* | *Bidding* |  |  |  |
|---|---|---|---|---|
| 3 NT by West | W | N | E | S |
| Lead: ♡ 3 | 1◇ | 1♡ | 2♣ | No |
|  | 2◇ | No | 2♠ | No |
|  | 2 NT | No | 3 NT |  |

West takes South's ♡ Q with his ace at Trick 1. He has eight top tricks. The ninth must be a long Diamond. The only danger is that South might hold four of the suit so West must play to counter that possibility. He plays the ♠ J and puts the ace on it. Immaterial here, such plays may suggest to both defenders that the other holds the queen. It is a legitimate ploy but the cards must be played smoothly. To play the knave, pause, apparently considering, and then play the ace is unethical and so inadmissible. A player may deceive the opponents by card-play; not by mannerism.

Now comes a small Diamond from the table, South playing the seven. Please check that West must duck this. Against five Diamonds with South the hand will not be made. West ducks because that seven is the lowest card held by the defence so, if North has one, he is forced to overtake. With North on lead the ♡ J is protected and the contract safe.

Perhaps South slipped when he played that seven from J 10 8 7. But he did not know where the nine was. If West had it and needed only four tricks in Diamonds it would need the play of the ten to prevent him ducking, but that would expose the knave to a finesse on the third round. That would give the contract away if West actually needed five tricks in the suit. There was no guarantee of anything as far as South was concerned but he still slipped. Maybe he could not afford the ten but he certainly could afford the eight.

## Timing

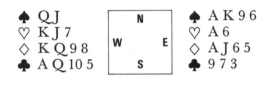

♠ Q J
♡ K J 7
◇ K Q 9 8
♣ A Q 10 5

♠ A K 9 6
♡ A 6
◇ A J 6 5
♣ 9 7 3

*Contract*
6 NT by West
Lead: ♠ 2

The lead appears to be from a four-card suit but that can be tested during play. If it is, the contract is safe provided that North does not hold four Diamonds as well. Please check. We need to arrive at a position where a trick taken by North forces him to give the contract whatever he returns. The Spades are unblocked and followed by three rounds of Diamonds; ending in dummy in order to cash the remaining two Spade tops on which West will discard a Club and *his last Diamond* (which is why only three should be played). The position will be:

♠ none
♡ K J 7
◇ none
♣ A Q 10

♠ none
♡ A 6
◇ J
♣ 9 7 3

A Club is now finessed, preferably the ten as that gives the chance for an overtrick. North is on play, and must lead a Heart or a Club. If a Club, the extra trick is given at once; a Heart is run to the knave, dummy entered via the ace to cash the last Diamond, discarding the ♣ Q, and the ♣ A is the entry for the last Heart.

## Gentle restraint

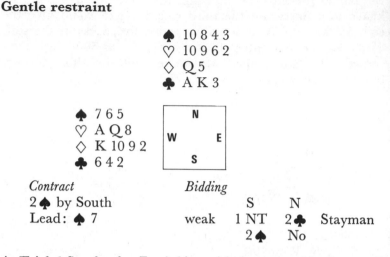

♠ 10 8 4 3
♡ 10 9 6 2
◇ Q 5
♣ A K 3

♠ 7 6 5
♡ A Q 8
◇ K 10 9 2
♣ 6 4 2

| *Contract* | *Bidding* | | |
|---|---|---|---|
| 2♠ by South | | S | N |
| Lead: ♠ 7 | weak | 1 NT | 2♣  Stayman |
| | | 2♠ | No |

At Trick 1 South takes East's king with the ace and leads a small
Diamond towards dummy's queen. What should West do? He
may not make his king if he ducks. Nevertheless he should, for
if South has the ace the contract is cold with four Spades, two
Diamonds and two Clubs. The defenders need one Club, two
Diamonds and three Hearts to beat the hand. If South has the
◇ J and the king is played he can establish a Diamond trick
for a Club discard. So the play is ◇ A by East and follow
partner's defence with a second trump. West takes the next
Diamond and plays a third trump. Now if South can go down
he will.

The inexperienced player is often too quick to play a winning
card in what is superficially a dangerous situation. Often enough
what looks like a disastrous play is actually harmless.

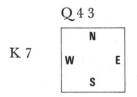

Q 4 3

K 7

West has led the king, finds queen to three in dummy and
South takes the trick with the ace. Yet if East happens to have

the knave nothing at all has been lost. In fact if East badly needs an entry the situation may prove most favourable.

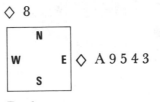

♦ 8

♦ A 9 5 4 3

Declarer

South plays in 4♡ having opened 1♦. The single ♦ 8 comes from the table. The inexperienced player plays the ace almost automatically. Yet there is no danger that it will run away. South must have five cards in Diamonds and dummy cannot trump four of them. If South started with K Q J 10 to five the play of the ace practically gives the hand away. Duck, and South wins with an honour but East still stops the suit twice so South must not only use one of dummy's trumps but must at some point concede the ace as well.

**Tactical traps**

♠ A 7 6
♡ K Q J 6 4
♦ K Q 6
♣ J 9

♠ K Q J 5
♡ A 7
♦ 9 5
♣ A Q 5 4 3

*Contract*
6 NT by West
Lead: ♡ 10

A contract of 6♡ might have been better but no better against the same lead. West now had to choose between playing South for the Diamond ace or taking the Club finesse. One round of Diamonds was necessary of course and, coming at Trick 2, the king won. West was faced with the same problem, decided to believe North, and so entered dummy with a Spade to play another Diamond. The queen lost to the ace and a second trump came. With the Club king wrong, that was one down.

*But such things can work both ways:*

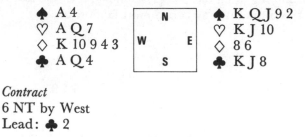

```
♠ A 4              ♠ K Q J 9 2
♡ A Q 7            ♡ K J 10
◇ K 10 9 4 3       ◇ 8 6
♣ A Q 4            ♣ K J 8
```

*Contract*
6 NT by West
Lead: ♣ 2

The duplication of shape was unfortunate, four top Clubs and five top Hearts worth only six tricks, and no finesse position, no end-play possible; all hinged on the position of the ◇ A. West took Trick 1 in dummy and played a Diamond to his king. North ducked it. In his mind was the idea that if he took the trick declarer might get home by a finesse in Hearts. If he ducked declarer might rely upon the ◇ A being with South. Who knows how to handle such situations? Anyone can go wrong so anyone who does go wrong should not worry too much about it. Worse mistakes are more common.

## The obligatory finesse

This finesse wins the contract whether it itself wins or loses.

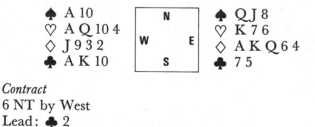

```
♠ A 10             ♠ Q J 8
♡ A Q 10 4         ♡ K 7 6
◇ J 9 3 2          ◇ A K Q 6 4
♣ A K 10           ♣ 7 5
```

*Contract*
6 NT by West
Lead: ♣ 2

South produces the Club queen and West wins the trick. There are now eleven top tricks but a certainty of making twelve with anything like reasonable distribution. West eliminates Diamonds from the opponents' hands, plays ace, king and a third Heart and finesses the ten. If this wins it is the twelfth trick. If it loses, South having followed of course, North has only black cards left and must concede the extra trick, either by playing into the Club tenace or through the pinning Spades.

### End-plays also come in the middle

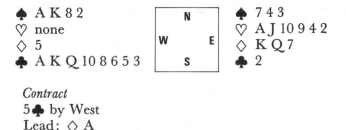

♠ A K 8 2
♡ none
◇ 5
♣ A K Q 10 8 6 5 3

♠ 7 4 3
♡ A J 10 9 4 2
◇ K Q 7
♣ 2

*Contract*
5♣ by West
Lead: ◇ A

The defence is horrifyingly accurate, taking the ◇ A and switching to a Spade. This declarer drew three rounds of trumps and continued trumps, hoping for a helpful discard. None came. None could do so reasonably. Declarer was marked with eight trumps and one top Spade while three good tricks were on the table. Either he should be claiming twelve tricks or he was void of both red suits. The defence therefore had no problem; no hope either, for the only distribution to beat this hand now is for one of them to hold the three outstanding high Spades, Q 10 9. The actual position was:

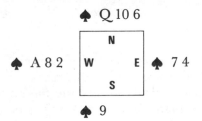

♠ Q 10 6

♠ A 8 2    ♠ 7 4

♠ 9

and the lead of a small Spade towards dummy's seven must succeed. North cannot afford to overtake South's nine while if South is allowed to win the trick he has only red cards left.

## Simplicity with early pressure

Normal play in no-trumps is to establish the necessary number of tricks and then cash them. Sometimes however we can afford to cash a few at an early stage. The basic criterion here is that no trick of length should be established for the opposition.

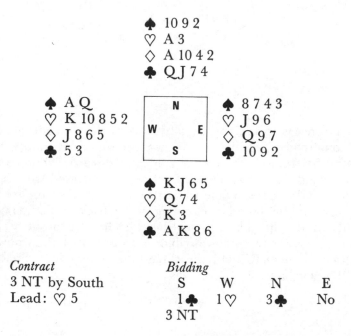

```
                    ♠ 10 9 2
                    ♡ A 3
                    ◊ A 10 4 2
                    ♣ Q J 7 4

♠ A Q              ┌─────────┐        ♠ 8 7 4 3
♡ K 10 8 5 2       │    N    │        ♡ J 9 6
◊ J 8 6 5          │ W     E │        ◊ Q 9 7
♣ 5 3              │    S    │        ♣ 10 9 2
                   └─────────┘
                    ♠ K J 6 5
                    ♡ Q 7 4
                    ◊ K 3
                    ♣ A K 8 6
```

| *Contract* | *Bidding* | | | |
|---|---|---|---|---|
| 3 NT by South | S | W | N | E |
| Lead: ♡ 5 | 1♣ | 1♡ | 3♣ | No |
| | 3 NT | | | |

The lead runs to South's queen and he sees eight top tricks. If he can find the Spade queen with East a ninth can be established before the Hearts are cleared. Once the bidding is considered however it is more than likely that West has both top Spades. South therefore procrastinates, playing off his Clubs to see if anything happens. It does. West has to throw two Diamonds so South plays on Diamonds and establishes his ninth trick without trouble.

## Defensive block

Simple arithmetic discovers the obvious, and it's brilliant.

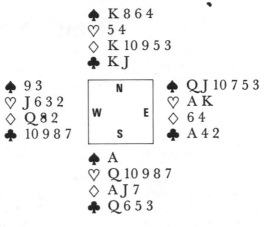

♠ K 8 6 4
♡ 5 4
◇ K 10 9 5 3
♣ K J

♠ 9 3
♡ J 6 3 2
◇ Q 8 2
♣ 10 9 8 7

♠ Q J 10 7 5 3
♡ A K
◇ 6 4
♣ A 4 2

♠ A
♡ Q 10 9 8 7
◇ A J 7
♣ Q 6 5 3

*Contract*
3 NT by South
Lead: ♠ 9

## Teams of four

South wins Trick 1 and successfully runs the Diamond knave. He then plays a Club to dummy's king, won by East's ace.

In Room I East cashed the ♡ K to tell partner of his sure entry and then cleared the Spades. That looked pretty automatic but it should be checked—please.

In Room II East counted tricks. Five Diamonds, two Clubs and two Spades added up to nine. So to play Spades would enable South to cash nine tricks at once. Now, when a player has a set number of tricks, the only way to stop him making them is to sever his communications, either to cut him off from certain tricks or to contrive a blockage. It was useless then to return a Club because that would not block the suit—it would unblock it. There being only one suit left, East played it—a Diamond.

Declarer was now completely frustrated. If he took the Diamond in his own hand he could never get back to cash his ♣ Q. If he took it in dummy he blocked the suit. The hand can actually be made by clearing Clubs before touching Diamonds, risking to go four down if the finesse failed. Thinking in defence produces results an astonishing proportion of the time by process of elimination. If neither this nor that is any use, then do what is left. It cannot be wrong to try.

# Routine Signals

## Standard leads and plays

From any doubleton lead the high card.

From three small cards lead the highest. Top of nothing. (Note: a not uncommon variation of this lead is to lead the middle card, MUD—middle, up, down. On the second round of the suit a higher card shows that the lead was from three; a lower card denotes an initial doubleton. The argument against top of nothing is that it reveals too much to declarer. The argument against MUD is that the play of a higher card on the second round is confusing to partner as this is the normal expectation when leading from a picture.)

From unsupported pictures lead low from three or four cards, the fourth highest from any longer holding.

(Note: some first-class players often lead an indeterminate card from unimportant holdings, trusting their partner to read the distribution—and trusting the declarer not to. This habit should be eschewed by players not yet at that level of ability.)

*Aces*: Against suit contracts seldom lead an ace and even less frequently lead away from it. The exception to this is the lead of a suit partner has bid; then always lead the ace. If a suit containing an ace simply has to be led, then the standard play is the ace. Against no-trumps contracts the standard lead from a suit containing the ace will be the fourth highest card, again with the exception of partner's suit. This fourth highest is the standard lead against no-trumps—the suit being the one in which we hope to establish length. A J 8 *6 4*   K Q 9 *7 4*  K 10 8 *6 4* 2 etc.

From suits with good sequentials lead the top card of the sequence: Q J 10 9 3   J 10 9 8 4   10 9 8 5 etc.

Sometimes the top of an interior sequence is a good lead. A *Q J* 10 6   K *J* 10 8 4   Q *10* 9 3 2 etc.

## Lead from A-K and others

Against no-trumps the lead from A K to four or more will be the fourth highest. Against suit contracts this is of course out of the question. We may establish length in a no-trump contract and then cash any aces and kings. But at suit contract tricks are taken on the first and second round of suits, sometimes the third, "never" the fourth for then our winners are trumped. So with holdings such as A K, K Q, A K 5 4, K Q 7 we must lead honours, either taking the trick or, losing it, establishing a card as a winner for the second round.

The lead from A K and others traditionally was the king, the same card as was led from K Q and others. Many players still play that way. But even in 1937 we were playing the ace from this holding and gradually over the years it has come to be recognised as the standard lead. It should be so because it is more efficient. There are various situations where it gives a genuine advantage. The most common is when the declarer attempts a Bath Coup.

```
7 5 4
      ┌─────────┐
      │    N    │
      │ W     E │  9 2 or J 9 2
      │    S    │
      └─────────┘
```

West leads the king, playing it from A K and others or K Q and others. With 9 7, if we think it is from A K we play the nine, an encouraging card, hoping that the ace will follow and we will be able to trump the third round of the suit. We find that the lead was from K Q and a continuation finds declarer with A J and another, thus making two tricks in the suit when entitled to only one. Holding J 9 2 we may fear that a continuation will establish a trick for declarer who may hold queen to three. We discourage, only to discover that the declarer has the ace to three and only a continuation would break the hand, establishing a second trick in the suit for us immediately. None of these troubles arise with the lead of the ace. We encourage with 9 2, discourage with J 9 2 and do the opposite if the lead is the king.

There are other positions also as, for example, in a slam contract where partner leads the king of our void. Playing king from A K we do not know whether to ruff or not.

The lead of ace from A K and others applies to the opening lead only. During the play of the hand at a later stage the success of a led king gives an indication of the position of the ace while there is usually plenty of evidence from both the bidding and the preceding play to aid us. The lead of an ace in the later play more often asks for information than needs to give it.

With A K alone the cards are played in reverse order, king first to denote no more of the suit. If you normally lead the king from A K, then the ace first denotes a doubleton.

### The rule of eleven

The lead of the fourth highest is not arbitrary. We could play a Rule of twelve and lead the fifth highest but often enough we are not dealt five cards; we could play a Rule of ten and lead third highest but this could waste a card which might have promotable potential. So, as we are leading mainly from length, the fourth highest is the most convenient and the Rule of eleven is forced upon us.

*Drill:* Take the pip-value of the card from eleven. The answer gives the number of cards higher than the led card which are outside the hand of the leader.

Q 8 6

```
               N
leads: 5   W       E   K 9 2
               S
```

Five from eleven gives six cards higher outside the leader's hand. East can see five of them so declarer has only one. This enables East to play the nine, retaining his guard over dummy's queen.

The lead of a singleton against suit contracts is often success-ful, enabling us to obtain a ruff and perhaps more than one at an early stage. It is of doubtful value if it adversely affects our holding in trumps. From a hand containing queen to three trumps it is frequently better to lead our long suit, hoping to shorten declarer's holding in trumps by forcing him to ruff.

**Plays during play**

```
              Q 3 2
            ┌───────┐
            │   N   │
 K J 9 5    │ W   E │   A 6 4
            │   S   │
            └───────┘
             10 8 7
```

West, to take all four tricks, leads the knave.

```
              J 7 5
            ┌───────┐
            │   N   │
            │ W   E │   A Q 10 9
            │   S   │
            └───────┘
              K 6 4
```

East, to establish three tricks over dummy, leads the queen.

```
              K Q 9
            ┌───────┐
            │   N   │
            │ W   E │   A J 10 8
            │   S   │
            └───────┘
```

East, to establish three tricks over dummy, leads the knave.

```
              K Q 8
            ┌───────┐
            │   N   │
            │ W   E │   A 10 9 2
            │   S   │
            └───────┘
```

East, to establish three tricks over dummy, leads small, playing his partner for the knave.

## Finesses, odds-play, safety-plays

| W | E | |
|---|---|---|
| K 4 | 3 2 | To take one trick play small towards king. |
| Q 4 3 | 5 2 | Play small twice towards queen. |
| Q 4 3 | A 6 5 | To take two tricks play ace, then small towards queen. |
| Q J 4 | 5 3 2 | To take one trick play small twice from East. |
| Q J 4 3 | A 6 5 | To take three tricks play ace and then small twice towards West. |
| K Q 6 | 5 4 3 | To take two tricks play small twice from East. |
| K Q J 6 | 5 4 3 | To take three tricks play small three times from East. |
| K Q 4 3 | J 5 2 | |
| K J 4 3 | Q 5 2 | |
| Q J 4 3 | K 5 2 | To take three tricks play small twice from East. |
| K 4 3 2 | Q 7 6 5 | To take three tricks play small to either honour and then small from both hands. |
| A Q | 3 2 | To take two tricks play small to queen. |
| A Q 3 | 4 2 | To take two tricks play ace, later small to queen. |
| A Q 9 | 3 2 | To take two tricks play small to nine, later small to queen. |
| J 9 4 | Q 3 2 | To take one trick play small to nine. |
| A Q 10 6 | 9 5 3 | To take maximum tricks play small to ten, later small to queen. |
| A K J | 4 3 2 | To take three tricks play one top, then small to knave. |
| A K 4 3 | J 5 2 | To take three tricks play one top, then small to knave. |
| A Q 10 | 4 3 2 | To take three tricks play small to ten, later small to queen. |
| A Q 10 5 | 4 3 2 | To take four tricks play as above. |
| A J 10 | 4 3 2 | To take two tricks play small to ten, later small to knave. |
| K J 3 | 5 4 2 | To take maximum tricks play small to knave, later small to king. |

| W | E | |
|---|---|---|
| K 10 2 | Q 4 3 | To take two tricks play small to ten. |
| A 10 2 | Q 4 3 | To take two tricks play small to ten. The bidding may, however, have placed the king. Then play ace and small to queen. |
| A J 2 | 5 4 3 | To take two tricks play small to knave. |
| A K 10 | 4 3 2 | To take three tricks play small to ten. |
| A J 9 | 4 3 2 | To take two tricks play small to nine, later small to knave. |
| A K J 2 | 5 4 3 | To take three tricks play ace and king, later small to knave. For four tricks play small to knave. |
| Q 10 2 | 5 4 3 | To take one trick play small to ten, later small to queen. |
| K 10 2 | 5 4 3 | To take one trick play as above. |
| K 10 | A 9 5 2 | To take three tricks play small to ten. |

To lose no trick with

| | | |
|---|---|---|
| J 8 5 4 3 | A Q 9 6 2 | Lead knave. |
| Q 8 6 4 | A K 9 5 3 | Lead queen. |
| 9 6 3 | A K J 7 4 | Lead ace, later small to knave. |
| A 10 5 3 | K Q 9 6 3 | Lead king or queen. |

To lose one trick only with

| | | |
|---|---|---|
| A 10 4 3 | K 9 6 5 2 | Lead small to nine or ten. |
| 8 6 4 | A Q 9 7 2 | Lead ace, later small to queen. |
| K 9 5 | A J 8 6 2 | Lead ace, then small to nine. |
| A 7 5 | K 10 6 4 3 | Lead ace, then small to ten. |
| 10 6 4 | A K 8 5 3 | Lead ace, then small to ten. |
| K J 7 | A 9 6 5 4 | Lead king, later small to knave. |
| K 7 5 3 | A 10 9 2 | Lead king, then small to nine. |
| 8 6 2 | A Q 10 7 5 3 | Lead ace, later small to queen. |
| A 9 6 5 4 3 | J 2 | Lead small to knave. Knave remaining, later lead and run it unless covered. |
| 7 5 3 | A K 9 8 4 | Lead ace, then small to seven. (An adverse singleton is odds-on to be an honour.) |

Q 10 8     A 9 6 5 2     Lead ten and run it, later lead queen and run it.

To lose two tricks only with
K Q 8 7 6 4 2   5     When leading from the long hand lead small.

## Ruffing finesses

none   K Q J 10     Three extra tricks may be made here if South holds the ace. The king is played, run if not covered and the suit continued until the ace appears and is ruffed. Two or three tricks are available if North holds the ace. The king is run and loses leaving three extra tricks. If a genuine loser was discarded on the king this is worth three tricks, if not it is worth two extra.

4     A Q J 10     Play the ace and run the queen similarly. Two tricks are now established in the East hand.

none   Q J 10 9     Run the queen discarding a genuine loser if possible. Later run the knave, ruffing if covered. Two extra tricks remain.

4     A J 10 9     Play ace, then run the knave, later run the ten, establishing the nine.

none   A K J 10     Play ace king and either ruff out queen or decide to run the knave. Bidding and previous play are indications to right action.

## Covering honours

The basic principle throughout such situations is to cover a led honour if by doing so a card of our side may be promoted. If there is no possibility of this, do not cover.

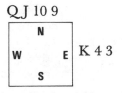

Q J 10 9

K 4 3

The queen is led from dummy. There is no possible gain to be made by covering this. The only cards which can be promoted belong to the opponents.

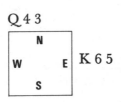

Q 4 3

K 6 5

West may now hold 10 8 6 and his ten be promoted if the queen lead is covered. The bidding must be kept in mind in all such situations. We do not cover if South has shown length in the suit. West could have a singleton—the ace?

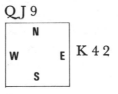

Q J 9

K 4 2

Cover the second, not the first honour led. To cover the first could find the whole position

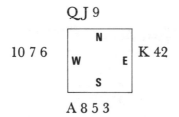

Q J 9

10 7 6        K 42

A 8 5 3

and a second finesse position be set up against partner's ten.

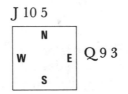

J 10 5

Q 9 3

Cover the second honour.

J 10 5

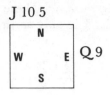 Q 9

Cover the first because the drop of the nine exposes the situation too clearly. Were it a small card it could well be better not to cover.

## Over- and under-ruffing

It is a common mistake of the inexperienced player to ruff to his later discomfort. The over-ruff is always tempting but should always be considered in the light of possible promotion.

With a holding such as A 10 2 to over-ruff a knave is to lose a trick. The remaining 10 2 will fall on declarer's K Q and one trick only is made, a trick which could be made at any time. Similarly with K 10 2 to over-ruff a knave is to make one trick only. Refuse to over-ruff and the small card goes on the ace, leaving us with K 10 over declarer's queen. With Q 9 3 it may well be wrong to over-ruff a ten. Declarer may have A J 10, partner the singleton king.

Occasionally it may be right to under-ruff.

♠ none
♡ K Q 7 4
◇ 8
♣ A K 8 6

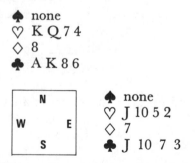

♠ none
♡ J 10 5 2
◇ 7
♣ J 10 7 3

North is dummy, Diamonds are trumps and declarer, South plays a Spade and ruffs with dummy's eight. To discard a Club or Heart may establish a vital trick for the declarer. The small trump is no use. Declarer is going to return to hand with— probably—the Heart ace and draw that trump. Under-ruff and

no trouble can ensue. The long cards in dummy are now useless
for East will simply follow dummy's discards.

**Standard false-carding**

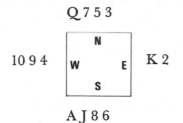

A J 9 8 4 3

7 5 2         Q 10

K 6

North plays small to dummy's king. East may drop the queen
in order to induce North to finesse the nine on the next round.
If the ten is played instead North will probably drop the queen
for if the ten is single the queen cannot be caught.

Q 7 5 3

10 9 4        K 2

A J 8 6

North, dummy, leads the three, East playing small and the
knave wins. West plays the nine. South may now re-enter the
dummy to play the queen, hoping to pin the ten.

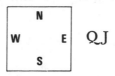

Q J

If declarer is thought to hold only eight cards in this suit the
queen may be played on the first round. In a trump suit a finesse
losing to the knave is now likely because of the danger of losing
trump control if West has four.

A Q 7 5 3

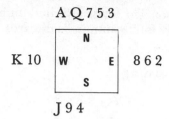

K 10   W      E   8 6 2

J 9 4

South, dummy, leads small and West may play the king. If this is a true card declarer must finesse the nine next.

A 9 5 4

7 5 3   W      E   Q 10 6

K J 8

North plays small to dummy's knave and follows with the king. East, known to hold the queen, must play it. There is no judgment here; the play is obligatory.

9 8 4 3

J 10 6   W      E   A 5

K Q 7 2

North, dummy, with no further entry, plays to the king which wins. West must drop the ten and now declarer may guess incorrectly.

A Q 4 3

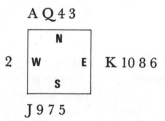

2   W      E   K 10 8 6

J 9 7 5

South finesses the queen. If East wins, the play of the ace on the next round will expose his ten to a marked finesse. He should play the eight. South may read this as 10 8 doubleton, return to hand and play the knave, thus losing two tricks.

Q 4

J 10 | W    E | A 7 2

K 9 8 6 5 3

South plays small to queen. East ducks. South may now play West for the bare ace.

Q 8 4 2

3 | W    E | J 9 6 5

A K 10 7

On South's ace East drops the nine. South may then play next the king.

False-carding comes under the heading of deceptive play. It should not be embarked upon if it can deceive the partner; only when solid tricks are at stake as above. The objective of the defenders should be to reduce the deal to double-dummy. Doing so may give information to declarer but he started with an advantage; making knowledge equal all round cancels that advantage. Nevertheless there are times when the declarer can be put to a disadvantage without adversely affecting either defender.

A J 9

K Q 3 | W    E |

Declarer leads small from South. His natural play with this holding is to finesse the nine, playing for the top honours to be split but for the ten to be with West. Therefore West should give him the opportunity to do precisely that, and so play small. The present distribution is against the odds. Declarer plays on odds. Don't stop him.

K Q 10 4

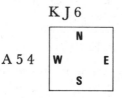

A 5 3

Declarer plays small to dummy's king. East should duck. Declarer may repeat the play. If East takes his ace on the first round the ten is almost certain to be finessed on the next round. Similarly, transferring ace to three to the West hand, West should duck twice, still leaving declarer to guess.

K J 6

A 5 4

When a small card comes from South West should almost always play small. If declarer has a singleton and guesses correctly, the ace is lost, yet, if it be played, the king is now established for the discard of a loser and nothing may be lost anyway.

The declarer has less frequent opportunity to false-card than have the defenders, not only because dummy cannot false-card and consequently he has only one hand against their two, but because defensive signals and deductions from the bidding may negate his efforts.

However, he should do what he can and at least he has no partner who can be deceived into a mistake by any false card he might play. Therefore when wishing to encourage or discourage a continuation of a led suit he should play exactly as if he were a defender. He has Q 6 3 and an ace is led, small from dummy and the seven from third hand. He should play the six. This may encourage the leader to continue with the king, only to find his partner had played his lowest from 10 8 7. If declarer does not wish the suit continued he should play low, from this time J 6 3. If third hand peters there is nothing to be done but occasionally third hand may produce the four which happens to be a singleton when the leader immediately has a problem to solve.

With a holding such as K Q 10 against third hand's knave, to win with the king may suggest to first hand that his partner holds the queen. At the worst he cannot guarantee that he does not hold it, something he most certainly can do if the declarer plays it.

Gilding the lily by winning with the ace from A K Q is likely to be counter productive when the knave comes from third hand. First hand may doubt that his partner holds K Q J. To take with the king is a better play. And may be in a situation such as Q 6 5 in dummy, A K J 2 with declarer and the ten comes from third hand. The play of the king may suggest the knave with third hand or even A J 10.

|  | | |  |
|---|---|---|---|
| ♠ A J 4 | **N** | | ♠ 8 5 2 |
| ♡ 6 4 | | | ♡ A 7 |
| ◇ J 10 4 3 | **W** | **E** | ◇ K Q 9 6 5 |
| ♣ K Q 9 4 | **S** | | ♣ A 7 6 |

| *Contract* | *Bidding* | | | |
|---|---|---|---|---|
| 3 NT by West | W | N | E | S |
| Lead: ♠ K | 1♣ | No | 1◇ | No |
| | 1 NT | No | 3 NT | |

The standard play with this A J and another holding is to duck the first round, permitting the king to win. North now cannot play a second round without giving a second trick and the defence's main suit may have been checked in its effort to become established. Here however we see that Spades are not the main danger. Hearts, that ace gone, are wide open for at least four adverse tricks. To take the first Spade however may be fatal should it have been from a five-card suit and the ◇ A be with South. Declarer therefore drops the ♠ J on the king, suggesting that he has the single ace left. That cuts off any five-card suit if South gets the lead with the ◇ A, as he almost certainly will, North being silent on the first round of bidding.

If a second Spade comes as it almost surely will, the ◊ A is knocked out and the contract secured.

A Q J 7 5

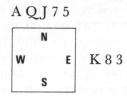   K 8 3

Declarer, South, takes a finesse in this suit. Dummy has no side entry so East should duck unless the actual trick is decisive. West's signal should have told him whether declarer has two or three cards in the suit. If two, a second finesse will ruin the hand. If three the suit cannot be cut off but declarer may be forced to expend an important entry in his own hand.

A J 10 8 6

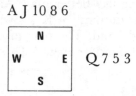   Q 7 5 3

A first round finesse of the knave should be ducked, keeping declarer, with no side entry to dummy, to three tricks instead of four. With a doubleton king West should play the king. When he doesn't play it he either hasn't got it or has made a serious mistake. His play of a small card technically marks South with king to three.

## Table of percentages for adverse distributions

| Adverse cards | will be split | % of deals | Adverse cards | will be split | % of deals |
|---|---|---|---|---|---|
| 2 | 1–1 | 52 | 5 | 3–2 | 68 |
|   | 2–0 | 48 |   | 4–1 | 28 |
|   |   |   |   | 5–0 | 5 |
| 3 | 2–1 | 78 |   |   |   |
|   | 3–0 | 22 |   |   |   |
|   |   |   | 6 | 4–2 | 48 |
| 4 | 3–1 | 50 |   | 3 -3 | 36 |
|   | 2–2 | 40 |   | 5–1 | 15 |
|   | 4–0 | 10 |   | 6–0 | 1 |

| Adverse cards | will be split | % of deals |
|---|---|---|
| 7 | 4–3 | 62 |
| | 5–2 | 31 |
| | 6–1 | 7 |
| | 7–0 | 0·5 |

## Table of percentages for shape of hands

| Shape | Approximate frequency % | Shape | Approximate frequency % |
|---|---|---|---|
| 4–4–3–2 | 22 | 4–4–4–1 ⎫ | |
| 5–3–3–2 | 16 | 5–5–2–1 ⎬ | 3 |
| 5–4–3–1 | 13 | 6–3–3–1 ⎭ | |
| 5–4–2–2 | 11 | 6–4–3–0 | 1·3 |
| 4–3–3–3 | 10 | 5–4–4–0 | 1–2 |
| 6–3–2–2 | 6 | 6–5–1–1 | 0·7 |
| 6–4–2–1 | 5 | 7–2–2–2 | 0·5 |

# Defensive Signalling

**The peter (high-low, echo, Lavinthal suit-preference)**

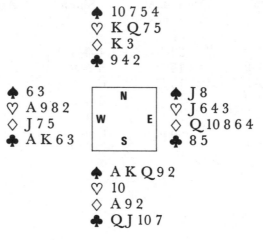

```
                ♠ 10 7 5 4
                ♡ K Q 7 5
                ◇ K 3
                ♣ 9 4 2

  ♠ 6 3                        ♠ J 8
  ♡ A 9 8 2         N          ♡ J 6 4 3
  ◇ J 7 5      W       E       ◇ Q 10 8 6 4
  ♣ A K 6 3         S          ♣ 8 5

                ♠ A K Q 9 2
                ♡ 10
                ◇ A 9 2
                ♣ Q J 10 7
```

*Contract*
4♠ by South
Lead: ♣ A

At Trick 1 East *peters* with the ♣ 8. Playing ace from ace king and others he does not have to wonder whether a peter might ruin the hand if the lead is from K Q. His eight, the play of an unnecessarily high card, is an encouragement, i.e.: a request for a continuation of the suit.

South, seeing that card and fearing a third-round ruff against him, drops the queen. This is bad play. Against a possible continuation declarer should play his lowest. West now, missing the seven and five, knows that this is a peter, so continues with the king. Had South dropped the seven, West would have missed only the five and might have wondered if South was false-carding from a holding such as Q 7 5.

A third round of Clubs is now trumped by East and he returns a Heart as instructed, enabling West to get the lead again and play a fourth Club, East over-ruffing the dummy to defeat the excellent contract by two tricks.

"As instructed" because West's third Club was specifically the six and East, missing the three, and appreciating that this six was the highest card West could play, returned a Heart as being the higher-ranking of the suits in which West might have a quick entry. Had West's entry been in Diamonds he would have played the three, not the six. (This is the Lavinthal suit-preference signal, and pretty useful sometimes, as we see.)

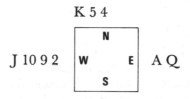

K 5 4

J 10 9 2    A Q

At Trick 1 West leads the knave. Dummy ducks, East perforce wins with the queen and then cashes the ace. West, aware of the exact situation, drops the ten. This obviously being the highest card he can play, East switches to the higher of the other suits (not trumps). West wins and plays the deuce of his original suit, allowing East to ruff dummy's king. Simple, effective and, with experience, automatic.

## "That" queen-play

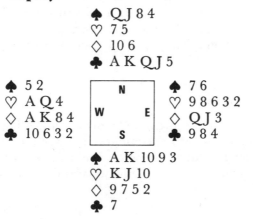

                    ♠ Q J 8 4
                    ♡ 7 5
                    ◇ 10 6
                    ♣ A K Q J 5

♠ 5 2                               ♠ 7 6
♡ A Q 4                             ♡ 9 8 6 3 2
◇ A K 8 4                           ◇ Q J 3
♣ 10 6 3 2                          ♣ 9 8 4

                    ♠ A K 10 9 3
                    ♡ K J 10
                    ◇ 9 7 5 2
                    ♣ 7

*Contract*
4♠ by South
Lead: ◊ A

On the lead of the Diamond ace, East, appreciating that West holds the king also, drops the queen. This is a standard play with a specific meaning: "I can take the next trick and I want to get the lead." West dutifully plays a small Diamond to East's knave and a Heart switch defeats the contract. The play is obvious to East as soon as he sees the dummy and, when West sees the Diamond queen, it is equally so to him.

### Discarding signals

The standard method of informing partner which suit to lead is the peter or echo, the play of an unnecessarily high card followed by one lower. If there is a choice of suits and a high card from the desired suit cannot be afforded, the lowest card of another suit may prove sufficient to give the necessary information. With a choice of discard from two suits this is normally adequate. Less common is the situation where there is a choice from three suits, as when a discard is made on a trump after a trump lead or when failing to follow at an early stage in no-trumps. Partnerships may arrange their own method for coping with this situation, rare though it may be. It may be agreed to discard from an unwanted suit a high or low card to designate which of the remaining two suits is desired. No method is infallible for we may be dealt a combination of cards which makes it impossible for the agreed signal to be used, the correct signal either giving away a trick or ruining an essential guard.

### Reverse peters

Used either in discarding or in following suit. A high card shows no interest, a low card encourages. The argument in favour of this method is that it is quite common to wish to signal encouragement yet be unable to afford a sufficiently high card.

A 8 7 4

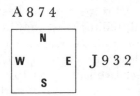 J 9 3 2

In the middle of a no-trumps contract, for example, our partner, West, suddenly switches to the king of this suit. To encourage would probably require the nine did we use normal peters, but this would almost certainly cost a trick by promotion of dummy's eight on the fourth round. Using reverse peters the play of the deuce encourages and all is well. Holding simply 9 3 2 East can drop the nine to discourage with little risk. This method is worth serious consideration but because traditional high-low signals are so ingrained and habitual with most players, for some time to come anyway it will tend to be agreed only by regular partners.

## Roman

This method uses an odd-pip card to encourage, an even-pip card to discourage. This may work well but there are clearly times when it may go wrong—e.g. when we wish to encourage but have been dealt only even cards.

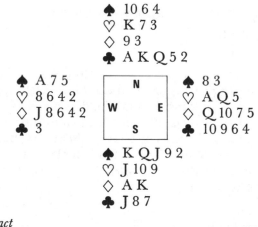

♠ 10 6 4
♡ K 7 3
◇ 9 3
♣ A K Q 5 2

♠ A 7 5
♡ 8 6 4 2
◇ J 8 6 4 2
♣ 3

♠ 8 3
♡ A Q 5
◇ Q 10 7 5
♣ 10 9 6 4

♠ K Q J 9 2
♡ J 10 9
◇ A K
♣ J 8 7

*Contract*
4 ♠ by South
Lead: ♣ 3

Reading the lead for a singleton East drops the ten as a suit-preference signal, telling West that his entry is in the higher of the relevant suits, i.e.: Hearts and Diamonds. West takes the first Spade and leads his lowest Heart, suggesting a return of the lower of the other two suits, perhaps gilding the lily somewhat. East wins, gives his partner a ruff and is put back with another Heart to give a second ruff. Two down. Without the signal at Trick 1 West might easily have switched to a Diamond after taking his trump ace.

```
                    ♠ 10 9 2
                    ♡ K 10 4
                    ◇ 7
                    ♣ K Q 10 8 4 2

    ♠ 7 2              ┌─────────┐       ♠ A 4 3
    ♡ A 8 2            │    N    │       ♡ 9 3
    ◇ K Q 10 4 3    W │         │ E     ◇ A 9 8 6 2
    ♣ 9 6 5           │    S    │       ♣ J 7 3
                      └─────────┘
                    ♠ K Q J 8 6
                    ♡ Q J 9 6 5
                    ◇ J 8
                    ♣ A
```

*Contract*
4♠ by South
Lead: ◇ K

East overtakes the ◇ K and switches to the ♡ 9. South plays the queen to preserve an entry in dummy. West, appreciating that South on the bidding does not hold as many as six cards in Hearts, and therefore his partner's lead cannot be a singleton, holds off, almost perforce as he has no other entry, but plays the ♡ 8 to encourage. When East obtains the lead with his trump ace he continues Hearts and a third round provides him with a ruff for the setting trick.

## Unorthodox leads as signals

West leads from K Q J to six against no-trumps. His entry

must be in one of two suits, dummy being pretty solid in the remaining one. Declarer holds off and West follows with the knave. Declarer holds off again and West plays the deuce, dropping the ace. Obviously he has indicated—twice—that his entry is the lower-ranking of the relevant suits.

## Giving the count by discarding

This may be done by playing low or high cards to show odd or even holdings. The standard situation is to play low to show three cards, high to show two. Completion of the high-low signal may confirm the play but frequently there is no time available.

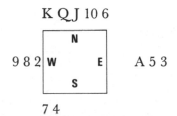

Dummy's entry having been removed by the opening lead, declarer can now be cut off and the contract broken by precisely one trick if East takes the second round of this suit. If he holds off until the third round the contract will be made. East however does not know this and must depend upon his partner's signal. West plays the two on the first round and East holds off. The king follows. East wins the trick, the eight from partner telling him of three cards and therefore only two with the declarer.

## Top of sequence plays

```
            Q 5 4
          ┌───────┐
          │   N   │
        W │       │ E    J 10 9 8
          │   S   │
          └───────┘
```

North plays a small card and East inserts the knave. This tells West the situation in that suit. He will know from the bidding that this knave cannot be a singleton, so, when East plays it, he must be able to afford to do so. Consequently he must have a sequence of lower cards equivalent to that knave.

A player marked with a number of cards in a suit suddenly discards the ace. He must be able to afford it. Therefore he must have the king plus the requisite number of sequential cards below to cover anything the opponents play. If dummy has four to the nine and he throws the ace, he must hold K Q J 10 as well. This type of play can be most helpful in no-trumps contracts where declarer is forced to use an entry into his hand. It will enable partner to continue that particular suit if necessary whereas otherwise he might have shied away from it simply because the declarer had voluntarily played it.

## Underlead as signal

    ♢ none
    ♣ A K Q 10 8 3 2

Holding this against a confidently bid contract of 6♠, the two of Clubs is led, the player deciding that the only way to defeat the contract is to obtain an immediate ruff in Diamonds. He takes the chance that his partner has the ♣ J. Did he wish to ruff a Heart he would have led the ♣ 8, the highest card he could afford which his partner would have to cover. The ten might be let go. The underlead can also come later:

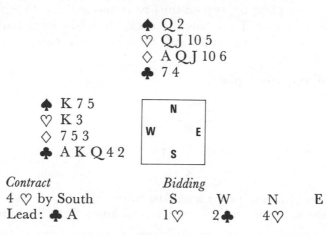

           ♠ Q 2
           ♡ Q J 10 5
           ♢ A Q J 10 6
           ♣ 7 4

♠ K 7 5
♡ K 3
♢ 7 5 3
♣ A K Q 4 2

| Contract | Bidding | | | |
|---|---|---|---|---|
| 4 ♡ by South | S | W | N | E |
| Lead: ♣ A | 1♡ | 2♣ | 4♡ | |

The moment dummy goes down the hand is double-dummy to West—bar one card. East has approximately nothing. Every missing honour must be with South to justify his opening bid. Any losers he has in Spades can be discarded on the long Diamonds. Only if East can be given the lead before trumps are drawn is there a chance to defeat the contract. So? So East must be given the lead. West plays a small Club, East wins with the knave and returns a Spade to get the hand one down. If South has the ♣ J he will have been given an overtrick, maybe two, but that is immaterial. One chance is there; it must be taken. This underlead is not, of course, a signalling underlead. No signal is necessary because there is only one possible suit for East to return.

### Breaking the ace rule

This brings us to an uncommon play; the underlead of an ace against a suit contract. Normally the play is tabu but occasionally hands crop up where there seems to be no good lead and the circumstances appear favourable. The player on the left—dummy-to-be—should preferably have bid no-trumps at some stage of the auction and the future declarer have bid in a manner to suggest that his hand is not freakishly unbalanced. Chances are now that the led suit will stand up for two rounds. The lead should be from ace to three, hoping to find king-knave on the table preceding a wrong guess by declarer. The danger here, even if all appears suitable, is that partner, holding the queen, will hug it to his bosom instead of playing it, believing that the ace is with declarer. The lead must therefore be standard, low from an unsupported picture. Partner sees this, knows from the bidding that it is not a singleton and, as only one picture is missing, realises that this lead must be from the ace. This orthodox lead does not help declarer for we make the same lead from queen to three or four.

It is a curious historical fact that Culbertson, giving the standard lead as being small from an unsupported picture, recommends a departure from this when deciding to underlead an ace. He suggests the 7 from A 7 2, the one card which is likely to deceive partner into thinking that the lead is top of nothing and so retain his queen. In a mass of meticulous data this stands out as something quite bizarre. We can hook up these underleads with the uppercut, i.e.: the play of a high trump when ruffing in order to force one higher from declarer and perhaps promote a lower card in partner's hand.

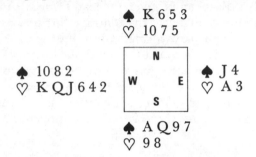

♠ K 6 5 3
♡ 10 7 5

♠ 10 8 2
♡ K Q J 6 4 2

♠ J 4
♡ A 3

♠ A Q 9 7
♡ 9 8

Spades are trumps. Clearly West-East have no genuine trick available in trumps. West leads the ♡ K overtaken by East's ace and the suit is returned. At Trick 3 West leads a small Heart on which East plays the ♠ J. This, forcing a top honour from South, automatically promotes West's apparently innocuous trumps into a sure trick. The third Heart from West may be employed also as a suit-preference signal for future reference. It should be basic routine, when holding useless trumps, to ruff with the highest available in the hope of embarrassing declarer (or dummy). The play may be made equally effective if the partner happens to lead a winning card against the dummy.

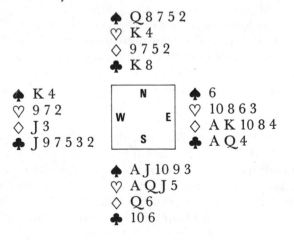

♠ Q 8 7 5 2
♡ K 4
◇ 9 7 5 2
♣ K 8

♠ K 4
♡ 9 7 2
◇ J 3
♣ J 9 7 5 3 2

♠ 6
♡ 10 8 6 3
◇ A K 10 8 4
♣ A Q 4

♠ A J 10 9 3
♡ A Q J 5
◇ Q 6
♣ 10 6

East opens 1 ◇ but South wins the contract at 3 ♠. West leads
the ◇ J and East takes it with the unorthodox ace, following
with the king. This reversal of normal play immediately alerts
West to the fact that the next card may be informative. When
East continues with the ◇ 4 West can read this as a suit-
preference signal, asking for the lead of a Club, should West
obtain the lead, rather than of a Heart. South ruffs with the ♠ 9
but West over-ruffs at once and returns a Club to defeat the hand.

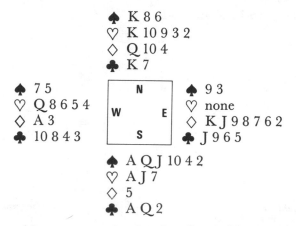

```
                 ♠ K 8 6
                 ♡ K 10 9 3 2
                 ◇ Q 10 4
                 ♣ K 7
  ♠ 7 5            N         ♠ 9 3
  ♡ Q 8 6 5 4   W     E      ♡ none
  ◇ A 3                      ◇ K J 9 8 7 6 2
  ♣ 10 8 4 3      S          ♣ J 9 6 5
                 ♠ A Q J 10 4 2
                 ♡ A J 7
                 ◇ 5
                 ♣ A Q 2
```

East opens with a pre-emptive 3 ◇ but South-North still reach
a small slam in Spades. East would like to make a Lightner
double, asking for an unusual lead against a voluntarily bid
slam, and probably would do so had the contract been of a
grand slam. But against the small slam he has to rely upon his
partner holding a sure trick, and this looks somewhat unlikely.
West however produces what may be one immediately, leading
the ◇ A, and East starts to wish that he had doubled. How then
can he make his partner lead a Heart to the disregard of anything else? A simple answer is there and East finds it with no
trouble. On the ◇ A he simply follows suit with the ◇ K,
establishing dummy's queen as a useless winner and alerting
partner to the fact that a lead of the higher relevant suit is
desired. West duly plays a Heart and the contract fails. Without
this switch it would of course have been made comfortably.
East would quickly be counted for seven cards in Diamonds,
two Spades and at least three Clubs, thus being marked with a
singleton Heart at the most.

# Flexibility

## Blocking and unblocking

```
        ♠ A K 4
        ♡ Q 5
        ◇ J 10 9 7 6 3
        ♣ 8 4
```

```
        ┌─────────┐      ♠ J 7 3
        │    N    │      ♡ J 10 9 6 4 2
        │ W     E │      ◇ A 2
        │    S    │      ♣ A 9
        └─────────┘
```

| Contract | Bidding | |
|----------|---------|---|
| 3 NT by South | S | N |
| Lead: ♣ 6 | 1♡ | 2◇ |
| | 2 NT | 3 NT |

West's Club is taken by East's ace and the nine returned, South playing the knave and West the queen. West now leads the two dropping South's king, by which time East has either beaten the contract or given it away.

On the lead of the third Club, which might be a suit-preference signal, East considers what entry West can have for his remaining three winners in the suit. South for his bid must have the ♠ Q, ♡ A K, ◇ K. That with his 4 points in Clubs only adds to 16 points. If he also has the Diamond queen there is nothing the defence can do to beat the hand. South will simply knock out East's ace and make five tricks in Diamonds plus a Club, two—no—at least three Spades and the Heart ace. So the only possible entry West can have is the Diamond queen. East therefore defeats the contract quite comfortably by discarding his ◇ A on the third round of Clubs. South can now make three Spades, three Hearts, one Club and one Diamond, no more.

*General unblocking should be routine play.* West leads a queen against no-trumps. East with king and one more should unblock at once, the exception being when the play would establish a lower card in dummy.

Trump holdings should always be kept flexible, manipulated according to the number of entries required by each hand. Take a simple trump combination: A K 3 2 opposite Q J 6 5 4. To play the ace and king to draw the adverse trumps leaves one hand unable to obtain an entry should it need one.

A trump suit A K 9 4 3 opposite Q J 10 8, with trumps breaking two-two, should be reduced to K 9 4 opposite Q 8. Now should trump entries be needed the lead can be passed to either hand twice, the 4 to the 8, the nine to the Queen; or the 8 to the 9, the Q to the K. Inexperienced players nearly always make the mistake of taking an early ruff with their lowest trump. A K J 10 6 2 opposite Q 5 4 3. That deuce should be retained, since an extra entry may be needed.

A K 8 2—Q 9 3. With the expectation that this suit is likely to break unevenly, 4–2 the ace should be played and the 9 unblocked. Then a small one to the Q will leave K 8 in a finesse position if required, the 9 which would have blocked the suit having been got rid of.

K 7

|   | N |   |        |
|---|---|---|--------|
| W |   | E | J 10 4 |
|   | S |   |        |

Against no-trumps West leads a small card of this suit. Dummy's king is played. East's knave should be unblocked. This may enable West to play small from the queen to East's ten in order to knock out the ace and certainly will avoid blocking the suit if East gets the lead. Remaining with J 10 alone could easily ruin the hand.

A simple holding of A K Q 5 4 opposite 10 9 8 3 requires three cards to be unblocked on the three tops. Otherwise the suit cannot be run.

Avoidance of blocking when finessing is important too.

A Q 10 4—J 9 2. Finessing against the king the 9 should be played, not the J. The 9 winning, the J is now played on the second round, putting the ten on it if not covered, and leaving the lead in the same hand for a third finesse. If we played the J on the first round the lead would be in the West hand after the second finesse.

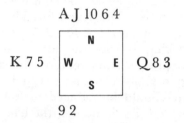

A J 10 6 4

K 7 5    Q 8 3

9 2

North, dummy, has no side entry so, when South leads the 9, West should play the king. If South holds queen to three it is dead anyway. The play cannot lose. The suit is not only blocked now but South may even be denied his ace. He may duck the king, hoping that West has both top honours. Then taking a second finesse which loses to the queen, South takes no trick at all in the suit.

## Deschapelles coup

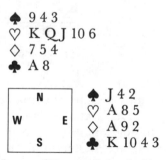

♠ 9 4 3
♡ K Q J 10 6
◇ 7 5 4
♣ A 8

♠ J 4 2
♡ A 8 5
◇ A 9 2
♣ K 10 4 3

South plays in 3 NT against a Diamond lead. East wins and immediately holds South to a maximum of two tricks in Hearts by playing his ♣ K, knocking out dummy's only entry. The ♡ A can now be held up until South has no more of the suit, East being informed by West's length-signal whether to take the second or the third round.

## Standard unblocking

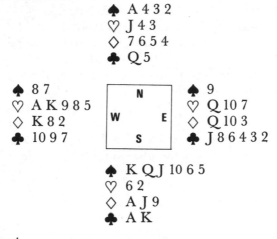

♠ A 4 3 2
♡ J 4 3
◇ 7 6 5 4
♣ Q 5

♠ 8 7
♡ A K 9 8 5
◇ K 8 2
♣ 10 9 7

♠ 9
♡ Q 10 7
◇ Q 10 3
♣ J 8 6 4 3 2

♠ K Q J 10 6 5
♡ 6 2
◇ A J 9
♣ A K

*Contract*
4♠ by South
Lead: ♡ A

East calls with the 10 and Hearts are continued, South ruffing the third round, eliminating Clubs and then drawing trumps in two rounds ending in dummy. Dummy now plays a small Diamond.

The position is:

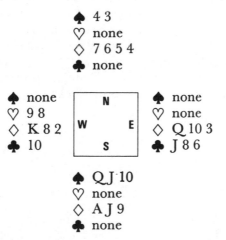

♠ 4 3
♡ none
◇ 7 6 5 4
♣ none

♠ none
♡ 9 8
◇ K 8 2
♣ 10

♠ none
♡ none
◇ Q 10 3
♣ J 8 6

♠ Q J 10
♡ none
◇ A J 9
♣ none

East must play the ◇ Q on this first lead of Diamonds from dummy. This blocks the suit and declarer must go one down. If he plays small the ◇ 9 will be finessed, taking West's ◇ K and West must either return a Diamond into South's A J tenace or give a ruff-and-discard, declarer ruffing on the table and discarding his ◇ J. This unblocking play, of course, depends upon the fact that dummy has no further entry. If there is another entry the defence is untenable; all that the defence can hope for is that declarer can be made to guess incorrectly. And if East plays low on the first Diamond there is no guess. So whether an entry is in dummy or not that queen should be played. The same play applies if it is the king.

7 4 3

|   | N |   |     |
|---|---|---|-----|
| W |   | E | K 5 |
|   | S |   |     |

South plays in a suit contract and, as above, has eliminated the side suits, leaving himself and dummy with this suit and trumps. North and South therefore have trumps, the defenders none. A small card, the 3, comes from North and the defence need two more tricks to break the contract. East must play his king at once. If he fails to do this he will be put on play with the second round of the suit and have no alternative to giving a ruff-and-discard. The result on the hand is immaterial. South may get home—he may not. One thing alone is sure—if East doesn't play that king, he will get home, so it must be played.

Sometimes a defender must be almost preternaturally alert to spot the danger of failing to unblock.

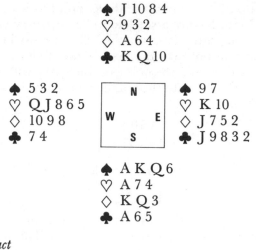

```
              ♠ J 10 8 4
              ♡ 9 3 2
              ◇ A 6 4
              ♣ K Q 10
♠ 5 3 2                        ♠ 9 7
♡ Q J 8 6 5      N             ♡ K 10
◇ 10 9 8      W     E          ◇ J 7 5 2
♣ 7 4                          ♣ J 9 8 3 2
                 S
              ♠ A K Q 6
              ♡ A 7 4
              ◇ K Q 3
              ♣ A 6 5
```

*Contract*
6♠ by South
Lead: ◇ 10

The duplication is most unfortunate for South yet he will still make this contract unless East does the right thing. The first Diamond is taken, two rounds of trumps only are drawn, the third being postponed for the moment lest a discard from one defender pass vital information to the other. South then plays the ♡ A. If East fails to unblock the king, the last trump will be drawn giving him another chance, as he luckily held only two trumps. If he fails to throw it, three rounds of each minor suit will eliminate both and then a second Heart to the king will force East to give a ruff-and-discard.

```
♠ Q 9 6 4         N          ♠ K 7 3
♡ A K 10 2                    ♡ J 5 4
◇ A J 10      W     E         ◇ 7 5
♣ Q 9                         ♣ K J 10 8 3
                  S
```

*Contract*
3 NT by West
Lead: ♡ 6

Dummy plays small and South drops the ♡ 7. West takes the trick with—of course—the ace. The drop of the ♡ 7 is strongly indicative that North holds the three, and has led from a five-card suit, South having a singleton. The essential point of the hand is that an entry to established Clubs must be available. The defence will not take the first round of clubs and now, if the ♠ A is with South, the only possible entry will be the ♡ J. If West wins Trick 1 with the ten, he will block the suit and the contract will fail.

A 10 4

K 5 2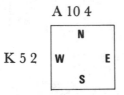

West leads the two of this suit against a no-trumps contract by South. East plays the eight, South the knave. This marks South with the queen (except if East is retaining it, but if so the subsequent play does not change). Later South plays the seven towards dummy's A 10. West should play the king. South, with Q 7, needing two entries to dummy, will play low to finesse the ten, preserving the ace as a second entry. (The fact that he plays like this almost certainly gives him the queen.) The play of the king by West reduces the number of entries to dummy, leaving the suit blocked, dummy with the ten, South with the single queen.

♠ 9 7 5 3
♡ Q J 10 4
◇ Q 9
♣ 8 6 4

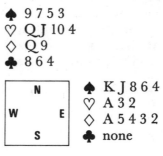

♠ K J 8 6 4
♡ A 3 2
◇ A 5 4 3 2
♣ none

*Contract*
3 NT by South
Lead: ◇ 6

South plays in 3 NT, bidding strongly despite East's opening bid of 1 ♠. East, seeing the lead, realises the approximate situation: South obviously has bid on a long, solid suit of Clubs, A Q of

Spades, the ♡ K and some rubbish in Diamonds. West would not lead from a mere knave to four, so he should have king to four, enough to beat this hand. South must have both top Spades, for West with one of them would have led such a useful filler. East therefore takes the ◇ A and, of course, plays the ♡ A before returning a Diamond. He sees that the Diamond suit is blocked and that West, on play with the fourth round and with no fresh information to guide him, could easily switch to a Spade instead of to a Heart, giving the contract.

```
                    ♠ 10 8 6 2
                    ♡ A K 5 4
                    ◇ 7 3
                    ♣ Q 9 2
   ♠ J 9 5           ┌─────────┐    ♠ K 7 4 3
   ♡ 10 8 6 3 2      │    N    │    ♡ J
   ◇ J 6 5           │ W     E │    ◇ A 9 8
   ♣ 8 5             │    S    │    ♣ A J 10 7 6
                     └─────────┘
                    ♠ A Q
                    ♡ Q 9 7
                    ◇ K Q 10 4 2
                    ♣ K 4 3
```

| *Contract* | *Bidding* | | | |
|---|---|---|---|---|
| 3 NT by South | W | N | E | S |
| Lead: ♣ 8 | — | — | 1♣ | Dbl. |
| | No | 2♡ etc. | | |

South reaches 3 NT after East has opened the bidding with 1♣. Dummy plays the nine, East the ten and South wins with the king. He enters dummy with a top Heart to lead a Diamond, East playing low, the king winning. South plays another Heart to the ace, intending to play another Diamond to establish the suit but on this East discards the ◇ A. All South can now do is take the Spade finesse and cash his tricks, going quietly one down.

(3 NT by North cannot be beaten. The contract could have been reached had South over 2♡ used a directional asking bid. 3♣ from him could have produced 3 NT from North. For DABs see my book: *Bidding Today*.)

**To draw or not to draw**

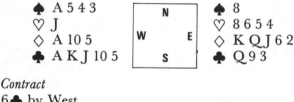

    ♠ A 5 4 3                   ♠ 8 2
    ♡ 7                            ♡ 9 6 3
    ♢ A 10 5                   ♢ K Q J 6 2
    ♣ A K J 10 5              ♣ Q 9 3

*Contract*
5♣ by West
Lead: ♡ A

North, winning Trick 1, leads a second Heart, ruffed by West.
West counts eleven tricks, five Clubs, five Diamonds, one Spade.
He draws trumps immediately and cashes those tricks. The
same hands are played in a contract of 5 ♢ by East. Lead: ♠ K.
East counts the same eleven tricks, takes the first Spade and
cashes those tricks. It is unnecessary that he try to ruff one of
his losing Hearts. He makes no extra trick by trying.

    ♠ A 5 4 3                   ♠ 8
    ♡ J                             ♡ 8 6 5 4
    ♢ A 10 5                   ♢ K Q J 6 2
    ♣ A K J 10 5              ♣ Q 9 3

*Contract*
6♣ by West
Lead: ♡ A

West ruffs the second round of Hearts. He counts eleven tricks
again—one short. The twelfth must come from a Spade ruff.
He plays ace and another, ruffing with the 9 or the Q. It
costs nothing to ruff high; had he ruffed small the higher card
would simply have fallen on one of his own high cards. But
somebody might have been dealt seven Spades and be in a
position to over-ruff. This is standard routine. If the power of

the trump suit remains unaffected we always ruff high even if
we know it doesn't matter. This is a habit which should be
formed so strongly that to depart from it would give us a mental
shock. Trumps are now drawn and the contract duly made.

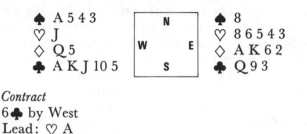

♠ A 5 4 3
♡ J
◇ Q 5
♣ A K J 10 5

♠ 8
♡ 8 6 5 4 3
◇ A K 6 2
♣ Q 9 3

*Contract*
6♣ by West
Lead: ♡ A

West ruffs the second Heart and counts ten tricks. Now therefore he needs to ruff two Spades in dummy. He plays ace and
another, ruffing high, returns to hand by playing dummy's
small trump and ruffs the second time with the Q. Back to hand
with the ◇ Q, draw the remaining adverse trumps and cash
Diamonds, discarding the last Spade on the third round. The
most important thing about dummy-play is to make the plan
before playing to Trick 1. Mistakes on this trick cost more than
do any other type. The procedure is: make the plan first. Then
carry it out. If something suddenly goes wrong—stop. Make a
second plan to cope with the changed circumstances and then
carry that out. If something else goes wrong—stop. Do the same
thing again.

Thought like this is seldom wasted. The inexperienced player
often fears to take time for forming his plan lest he annoy
opponents or appear to be less competent than he wishes to
appear. The inevitable result of this quite natural reaction is
that he plays too quickly, plays incorrectly, and finds himself
faced—although he does not appreciate this—with a problem
quite without solution, and wastes more time in trying to solve
the unsolvable than he would have done had he thought the
hand right through at the right time.

♠ 4 3 2
♡ A 8 6 2
◇ A
♣ A Q 10 9 7

♠ A 8 7 5
♡ 5
◇ K Q 8 6 3
♣ K J 8

*Contract*
6♣ by West
Lead: ◇ 2

Ten tricks on top so two ruffs in Hearts will suffice. We may also manage to establish Diamonds for a thirteenth trick. So—ace and another Heart. Ruff. Return to hand by overtaking a trump. We do not return by ruffing a Diamond, seeking to establish that suit on the way; we can do that next time. There is just the chance that some unpleasant defender might have been dealt all five missing trumps and to ruff a Diamond at this stage could prove fatal. So come back via a trump and North shows void. Stop. Someone did have all five. Ruffing the second Heart will leave us with no entry except by ruffing something else, so even six is now in danger and will be made only if South follows to two more Diamonds. So we ruff another Heart and then cash two Diamonds? No—there could be a Diamond discard on that third Heart. So we enter dummy with the ♠ A, cash two Diamonds, all following fortunately, ruff Diamond, ruff Heart and table our hand which now contains all winning trumps and one outside loser. Going back to Trick 4, we overtake a trump from dummy and both defenders follow suit. Nobody has five, somebody might have four but we can cope with that. Ruff second Heart, return to hand ruffing a Diamond—no need to cash winning Diamonds before trumps are drawn—draw the trumps, enter dummy with the ♠ A and cash Diamonds. If they break we make seven; if not we still make our contract of six. Not a good grand slam to be in at rubber bridge. At teams-of-four, yes, pretty good. The 4–3 Diamond adverse break is needed, but little more even on a Spade lead.

|  |  |  |  |
|---|---|---|---|
| ♠ Q 10 9 4 | | ♠ J 8 7 3 | |
| ♡ A K 5 2 | N | ♡ 7 4 | |
| ◇ K J 3 | W    E | ◇ A 6 4 2 | |
| ♣ 7 4 | S | ♣ J 10 5 | |

*Contract*
2♠ by West
Lead: ♣ A

The defence continues Clubs, West ruffing the third round. His plan is already made. Were it not made he would make it before ruffing that third Club. He has four tops in the red suits so needs four more tricks and plans to make them all by trumps. He plays two top Hearts and ruffs another with the 7, 8 or J, not with the 3. An over-ruff would now have to be by A or K. Now he plays A and K of Diamonds in that order, disdaining the finesse, and ruffs the last Heart, also high. He now has seven tricks and his hand still contains Q 10 9 of trumps to provide his eighth.

The defence changes. They start with three rounds of trumps. This reduces declarer to one ruff in Hearts so he makes his plan before playing to Trick 3, deciding in which hand he needs to win it. He must now make an extra trick from a red suit. He wins in dummy and finesses the ◇ J. If that wins he is home. It doesn't. The defence now play three top Clubs, removing his own last trump.

He is still home if the adverse Diamonds break 3–3, so he plays king and another to the ace. They fail to break so he goes one down, dummy's last two cards being a trump and a losing Diamond.

This was careless. He failed to take note of the fact that at Trick 3 one of the defenders discarded a small Heart. When he ruffed the third Club he should, before testing Diamonds, ruff a Heart. Suddenly he would have found that his fourth Heart had become the thirteenth and his ◇ K was still there to serve as an entry to it.

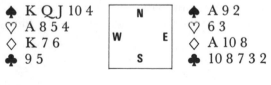

```
    ♠ K Q J 10 4    ┌─────────┐    ♠ A 9 2
    ♡ A 8 5 4       │    N    │    ♡ 6 3
    ◇ K 7 6       W │         │ E  ◇ A 10 8
    ♣ 9 5           │    S    │    ♣ 10 8 7 3 2
                    └─────────┘
```

*Contract*
4♠ by West
Lead: ♠ 3

Eight top tricks with the extra two from ruffing two Hearts in dummy. Unfortunately, however, the defence have different ideas and the hostile lead of a trump will surely be followed by another as soon as they regain the lead. The plan to ruff Hearts will therefore fail. The best—almost the only—chance now is to find a 3–3 break in the adverse Clubs. West takes Trick 1 and plays a Club, takes Trick 3 and plays another Club. Now the third Spade in dummy is an entry to play a third Club and ruff. If the suit breaks, two winning Clubs remain while the ◇ A provides the entry.

If the defence, fearing the Club break, switch to a Diamond, West can play a small Heart which forces the defence back to trumps.

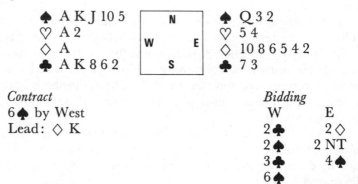

♠ A K J 10 5    ♠ Q 3 2
♡ A 2    ♡ 5 4
◇ A    ◇ 10 8 6 5 4 2
♣ A K 8 6 2    ♣ 7 3

| *Contract* | | *Bidding* | |
|---|---|---|---|
| 6♠ by West | | W | E |
| Lead: ◇ K | | 2♣ | 2◇ |
| | | 2♠ | 2 NT |
| | | 3♣ | 4♠ |
| | | 6♠ | |

A good 4♠ bid by East having already said twice that he has nothing. The one real danger here is that the Clubs might not break and that dummy, ruffing the third round, might be over-ruffed. West's plan therefore is not to ruff that third round. Taking Trick 1 he plays two top Clubs and, on the third, throws one of dummy's small Hearts. Now his own small Heart can be ruffed with a small trump without risk while, if the Clubs have failed to break, one of those can be ruffed with the ♠ Q.

## Cutting communications

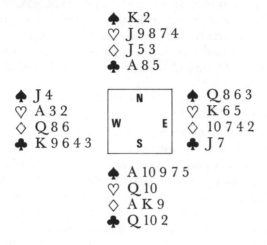

```
              ♠ K 2
              ♡ J 9 8 7 4
              ◇ J 5 3
              ♣ A 8 5
♠ J 4                        ♠ Q 8 6 3
♡ A 3 2          N          ♡ K 6 5
◇ Q 8 6      W       E      ◇ 10 7 4 2
♣ K 9 6 4 3      S          ♣ J 7
              ♠ A 10 9 7 5
              ♡ Q 10
              ◇ A K 9
              ♣ Q 10 2
```

*Contract*
3 NT by South
Lead: ♣ 4

Dummy plays small and South takes East's ♣ J with his ♣ Q.
He then attacks Hearts, but East wins the first round and returns
a Club, establishing West's suit before the second top Heart has
been knocked out. South goes down quite unnecessarily having
failed to appreciate that his ♣ Q 10 are the equivalent of the
♣ K once East produces the ♣ J. With the king he would
have ducked at Trick 1 to cut communications. He should have
done just that with the Q 10.

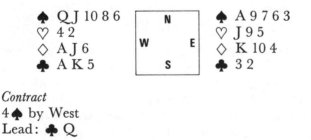

```
♠ Q J 10 8 6                ♠ A 9 7 6 3
♡ 4 2            N          ♡ J 9 5
◇ A J 6      W       E      ◇ K 10 4
♣ A K 5          S          ♣ 3 2
```

*Contract*
4 ♠ by West
Lead: ♣ Q

The instinctive reaction of the inexperienced player is to take
the trump finesse at Trick 2. As usual, the early play holds the

key and this is a hand where, providing the defence is not top-class, that trump finesse is not taken at all. The play at Trick 2 is a small Heart and, when in again, another. Now, unless the defence has attacked trumps, the ace is played, the losing Heart and Club ruffed and the defence is put on play with another trump, forcing a Diamond lead or the concession of a ruff-and-discard.

First-class defence may avoid this position when on lead after winning a trick in Hearts. Why should declarer play this way instead of drawing trumps of which he must have plenty? The danger of elimination and throw-in will instinctively present itself and a good defender, if North, will play a small trump—if he has a small trump. If South is on play he will continue Clubs and let North win the second round of Hearts. The defence may actually not be possible but, if it is, the top-class player will find it while West, faced with it, will realise that he will have to guess not only the Diamond situation but also the trump-position, without help.

**Basic counts**

|  | ♠ K Q J 6 4 2 | N | ♠ 10 5 |
|---|---|---|---|
|  | ♡ A 2 |  | ♡ K 8 6 4 |
|  | ◇ K J | W        E | ◇ 7 5 4 2 |
|  | ♣ J 5 2 | S | ♣ 10 8 3 |

| *Contract* | *Bidding* | | | |
|---|---|---|---|---|
| 2 ♠ by West | S | W | N | E |
| Lead: ♣ 4 | 1 NT | 2 ♠ | No | No |
|  | (13–15) | | | |

South wins Trick 1 with the ♣ K and plays the ace and another, North taking his queen and switching to a Heart, West's ace taking South's queen. A Spade goes to the ten, South winning and returning a Heart. With dummy's last entry gone, West plays a Diamond to the knave which might win or not, but the king won't because South's bid was 13–15 and if he held the ◇ A that would give him 17 points.

West with the same hand faces different bidding. Second-in-hand he opens 1 ♠ and all pass. The first four tricks are the same

but this time North wins the trump-trick and continues Hearts.
West plays a small Diamond to the knave. South cannot have
the ace or he would have opened the bidding.

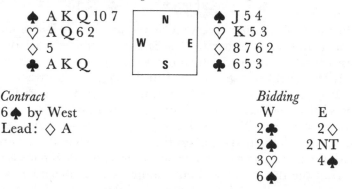

♠ A K Q 10 7       ♠ J 5 4
♡ A Q 6 2          ♡ K 5 3
◇ 5                ◇ 8 7 6 2
♣ A K Q            ♣ 6 5 3

| Contract | | Bidding | |
|---|---|---|---|
| 6♠ by West | | W | E |
| Lead: ◇ A | | 2♣ | 2◇ |
| | | 2♠ | 2 NT |
| | | 3♡ | 4♠ |
| | | 6♠ | |

West ruffs the second round of Diamonds and draws two rounds
of trumps, all following. The hand is basically simple; if Hearts
break three-three the contract is cold; if not, it *may be* one down.
Three rounds of Hearts follow. If they break, the last trump is
drawn. If they do not, there is still the chance that the outstanding trump is in the same hand as the four cards in Hearts.
If so, the fourth Heart is ruffed, West returns to hand, draws
the last trump and all is well.

♠ A Q 5            ♠ 9 6 3
♡ A J 4            ♡ 6
◇ K 7              ◇ A J 5 2
♣ A Q 8 6 5        ♣ K 10 9 4 3

Contract
6♣ by West
Lead: ♡ 2

West wins over South's ♡ K. This suggests that North holds the
♡ Q unless South is false-carding, deceiving his partner for no
apparent reason. If the play is orthodox, the contract should be
safe. West plans to eliminate Diamonds, with the extra chance
that the queen might fall in three, ruff one Heart and throw
North in with the ♡ Q to play into the Spade tenace. Trumps
are drawn, Diamonds ruffed out and the small Heart ruffed.
Leaving:

```
♠ A Q 5              ♠ 9 6 3
♡ J          N       ♡ none
◇ none    W     E    ◇ none
♣ 6          S       ♣ K 10
```

On the ♡ J dummy throws a Spade as soon as North covers. North must now either lead a Spade or concede a ruff-and-discard when dummy will throw a second Spade.

If West held the ♠ 8 instead of the ♠ 5 the contract would have been safe anyway, due to dummy holding the ♠ 9. Both red suits would have been eliminated and a Spade from dummy led to West's 8. North, winning, is end-played helplessly. If South covers the 8 West plays the queen. Two of three honours with the defenders have now gone and the Spade tenace is there to trap the third. But without dummy's 9 the defenders would have four cards of import and the play could only work if North had the lot.

## Standard elimination patterns

```
♠ A K 9 8 5          ♠ Q J 10 4
♡ K 5        N       ♡ A 6 4
◇ Q 5 3   W     E    ◇ A K 7
♣ A Q 9      S       ♣ 7 3 2
```

*Contract*
6♠ by West
Lead: ◇ J

The contract is unbeatable unless one opponent is void of trumps. If that happens, two finesses in Clubs must be taken, first the 9, then the Q. If both defenders follow to one round of trumps, all are drawn, the Hearts eliminated next, and then Diamonds, leaving the lead in dummy. The position is as before when a small Club is played towards West, he covering whatever South plays.

```
♠ A K 9 8 6          ♠ Q J 10 4
♡ K 6 4 2    N       ♡ A 8 7 5
◇ 4 3     W     E    ◇ J 7
♣ A 5        S       ♣ K 9 7
```

*Contract*
4♠ by West
Lead: ◇ 4

This contract is unbeatable unless one defender is void of trumps and the Hearts break 4–1. Both defenders following to one round of trumps, it is safe provided one defender's Hearts are not Q J 10 9. Trumps are drawn—the defence having cashed two Diamonds and switched to a Club—the odd Club is ruffed, eliminating the suit and a small Heart is played, ducking in dummy. This must be won by one of the sequentials, Q J 10 or 9. If Hearts were breaking they are now good; if not, either the defender on play must either lead away from his holding, thereby setting up a finesse position for declarer, or, having no more, must concede a ruff-and-discard, when the A and K are left for the last two rounds.

If on the lead of the first Heart, the first defender to play produces an honour, this is ducked equally. Barring that Q J 10 9 holding, the position is now untenable for the defence. Please check.

|  |  |  |
|---|---|---|
| ♠ J 10 9 | N | ♠ A 4 3 |
| ♡ K Q 8 6 4 | W E | ♡ A J 9 2 |
| ◇ Q 5 | | ◇ K 6 3 |
| ♣ A 5 4 | S | ♣ K 7 6 |

*Contract*
4♡ by West
Lead: ◇ 9

The lead runs to West's queen; he draws trumps in two rounds and plays another Diamond to South's ace. A third round comes and he ruffs. The hand is now over. Three rounds of Clubs leave one defender on play—immaterial which—and a Spade must now come; if from North, South is end-played after winning it, if from South, North's picture is immediately killed, leaving only one winner remaining.

The experienced player recognises these patterns as soon as he sees his dummy. The possibility of an end-play is there and he looks for the right sequence of play which will enable him to produce the right end-position. Change the Spades to J 4 3 opposite Q 5 2 with the danger of three losers and the same position is created to reduce those losers to two.

### Imperfect elimination

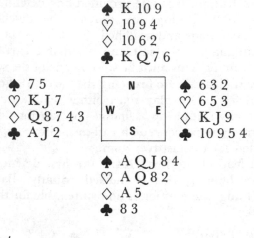

&spades; K 10 9
&hearts; 10 9 4
&diams; 10 6 2
&clubs; K Q 7 6

&spades; 7 5          &spades; 6 3 2
&hearts; K J 7        &hearts; 6 5 3
&diams; Q 8 7 4 3     &diams; K J 9
&clubs; A J 2         &clubs; 10 9 5 4

&spades; A Q J 8 4
&hearts; A Q 8 2
&diams; A 5
&clubs; 8 3

*Contract*
4 &spades; by South
Lead:  &diams; 4 Room I
&spades; 7 Room II

In Room II South was able to get his losing Diamond away on a Club. In Room I, however, he went down, the contract failing—we quote—*"against the killing lead of a Diamond"*. Yet the outline of a pattern is there and it might well have been aimed at. The opening lead is ducked, the second Diamond taken and a Club played, the king winning. South ruffs back a Diamond and plays another Club. West wins with the ace and exits with a trump, taken in dummy and the &clubs; Q played, South discarding a Heart. Noting the fall of the &clubs; J South sees the pattern appear, remains in dummy with another trump and runs the &hearts; 10 to West's knave. The position is:

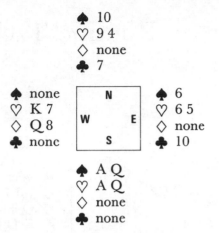

&spades; 10
&hearts; 9 4
&diams; none
&clubs; 7

&spades; none    &spades; 6
&hearts; K 7    &hearts; 6 5
&diams; Q 8    &diams; none
&clubs; nonc    &clubs; 10

&spades; A Q
&hearts; A Q
&diams; none
&clubs; none

and West has to lead. The situation is hopeless, and the contract is made. Which doesn't show much except that players can make mistakes when seeing 26 cards and bridge correspondents when they can see 52.

# 6    Routine Techniques

**Safety first**

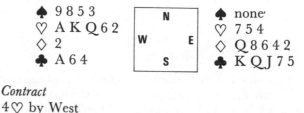

♠ 9 8 5 3          ♠ none·
♡ A K Q 6 2        ♡ 7 5 4
◇ 2                ◇ Q 8 6 4 2
♣ A 6 4            ♣ K Q J 7 5

*Contract*
4 ♡ by West
Lead: ♠ A

West trumped the lead, came to hand with the ♣ A, trumped another Spade and proceeded to draw trumps, intending to make twelve tricks—five Trumps, five Clubs and two ruffs. Unfortunately trumps broke 4–1 against him so he lost one trump, one Diamond and two Spades for one down. The play is good—providing that the contract is 6 ♡. In 4 ♡ it is not good. Correct play is to ruff the first Spade and then duck a round of trumps. The defence is then helpless and the contract is made with four trumps, one ruff and five Clubs. (The 4–1 break is a 28 per cent chance, and so is worth thinking about. The remaining dangers are 5–0 breaks (5 per cent) which will ruin the hand anyway, and so may be disregarded.)

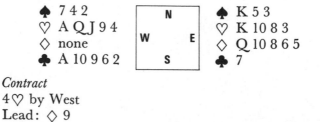

♠ 7 4 2            ♠ K 5 3
♡ A Q J 9 4        ♡ K 10 8 3
◇ none             ◇ Q 10 8 6 5
♣ A 10 9 6 2       ♣ 7

*Contract*
4 ♡ by West
Lead: ◇ 9

With a hand simply packed with losers it will be futile to try to establish a couple of winners by length. West must play a complete cross-ruff: ruff Diamond, play ♣ A and ruff Club, continuing ruffing Diamonds and Clubs alternately until he runs out of trumps. He makes nine tricks in trumps and one in Clubs. In the end-play he might manage to get a Spade trick but cannot afford to try for it earlier lest the defence lead a trump, reducing his trump tricks to eight.

*And:*

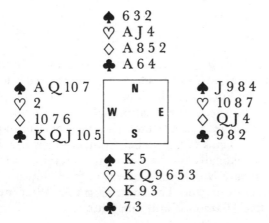

|  |  |  |
|---|---|---|
| ♠ Q J 4 | | ♠ A 9 3 2 |
| ♡ Q J 10 4 3 | | ♡ A 9 6 2 |
| ◇ none | | ◇ 9 6 |
| ♣ Q J 6 4 3 | | ♣ A 7 5 |

*Contract*
4♡ by West
Lead: ♣ 2

This lead can hardly be anything but a singleton. Play the ace and follow at once with ace and another trump, disdaining the finesse. South shows out on the second round. North wins and plays a Spade. Again the finesse is disregarded. North still has a trump left and must be given no chance to make a trick with it. Play the ♠ A then and draw the last trump. Declarer may now comfortably concede two tricks to the kings of Spades and Clubs.

## Avoidance

This is the denial of the lead to the dangerous hand.

|  | ♠ 6 3 2 |  |
|---|---|---|
| | ♡ A J 4 | |
| | ◇ A 8 5 2 | |
| | ♣ A 6 4 | |

| ♠ A Q 10 7 | N | ♠ J 9 8 4 |
|---|---|---|
| ♡ 2 | | ♡ 10 8 7 |
| ◇ 10 7 6 | W  E | ◇ Q J 4 |
| ♣ K Q J 10 5 | S | ♣ 9 8 2 |

|  | ♠ K 5 |  |
|---|---|---|
| | ♡ K Q 9 6 5 3 | |
| | ◇ K 9 3 | |
| | ♣ 7 3 | |

*Contract*
4♡ by South
Lead: ♣ K

West opens the bidding with 1♣ but South reaches 4♡. Viewing his dummy he sees four certain losers, one Club, two Spades—because the ♠ A must be with West—and one Diamond. It might be possible to establish a thirteenth Diamond but this depends upon finding not only an even break but an inability on the part of West to unblock the suit. If South eliminates Clubs and draws trumps nothing is more sure than that when he plays the ◇ K West will unblock his highest Diamond on it. South ducks the first Club and is pleased to note the two coming from East, suggesting that he is likely to hold three cards in the suit. The ♣ Q comes and South ducks that as well. The hand is now over. A Diamond is thrown on the Club ace, Diamonds are ruffed out and trumps are drawn, finishing with the lead in dummy where the established thirteenth Diamond takes care of one of South's Spades. (3 NT is of course safer but mostly unlikely to be reached.)

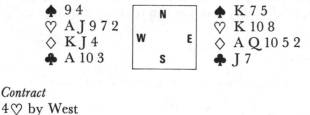

```
     ♠ 9 4              N            ♠ K 7 5
     ♡ A J 9 7 2                     ♡ K 10 8
     ◇ K J 4        W       E        ◇ A Q 10 5 2
     ♣ A 10 3           S            ♣ J 7
```

*Contract*
4♡ by West
Lead: ♣ 6

South produces the ♣ Q on the opening lead after dummy has played small. West can now establish an extra trick in Clubs by conceding the king, yet what could he do with it? It would be worse than useless, since it is vital that North not be permitted to gain the lead and attack that very vulnerable ♠ K. So West ducks at Trick 1, wins when South returns the suit and runs the ♡ 9, specifically the 9 as he wants to retain the lead and finesse again in case North holds queen to four. South takes the trick, but it doesn't matter. The contract is safe. West must take four Hearts, five Diamonds and one Club.

## Cross-ruff

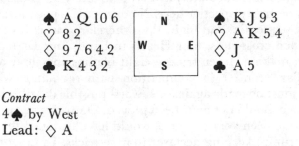

```
        ♠ A Q 10 6      ┌─────────┐      ♠ K J 9 3
        ♡ 8 2           │   N     │      ♡ A K 5 4
        ◇ 9 7 6 4 2     │ W     E │      ◇ J
        ♣ K 4 3 2       │   S     │      ♣ A 5
                        └─────────┘
```

*Contract*
4♠ by West
Lead: ◇ A

North switches to a Club at Trick 2 and West makes his plan. There is no complete cross-ruff because dummy has only two cards which can be ruffed back but there are plenty of Diamonds so he decides to ruff three of them in dummy. This should give him seven tricks in trumps and three tops outside. He therefore takes Trick 2 in his own hand and ruffs a Diamond, all dummy's trumps being high.

To return to hand he now needs to ruff a Heart but cashes the Club ace first. The basic rule for such contracts is to cash side winners as soon as possible. The danger in not doing so is that a defender may be able to discard on a suit which declarer is ruffing, and thus be able to ruff a winner which should have been cashed earlier, before he was given the opportunity to discard.

So two tops in Hearts and a Heart ruff and here is the one remaining danger, i.e.: that North may have started with two Hearts only and hold the ♠ 8, the one danger trump outstanding. But all is well—North follows, so it is second Diamond ruff, second Heart ruff, third Diamond ruff and the contract is safe. Four trumps in hand, three in dummy and three tops.

```
        ♠ Q 10 9 8      ┌─────────┐      ♠ A K J 7
        ♡ 4             │   N     │      ♡ A 9 8 6 5
        ◇ A 8 6 4 2     │ W     E │      ◇ J
        ♣ A 9 3         │   S     │      ♣ J 4 2
                        └─────────┘
```

*Contract*
4♠ by West
Lead: ♡ K

Here West does have a complete cross-ruff. Total cross-communication is immediately available to him with two singletons opposite their respective aces. No over-ruff is possible as all trumps are sequential and high. West therefore cashes his three aces and then cross-ruffs, four Hearts in hand, four Diamonds in dummy, making eleven tricks—eight trumps and three aces.

In a "Par" contest (a competition with set hands where every play must be made against the worst possible distribution), that Club ace should not have been played. One defender would certainly have been void of Clubs, would have trumped the ace and led a trump, keeping declarer to nine tricks. In practice it would be most unlikely for anyone with seven Clubs to K Q 10 to have remained silent during the auction. Nevertheless, once such dangers are known to exist, proper precautions should be taken in situations where they are less remote.

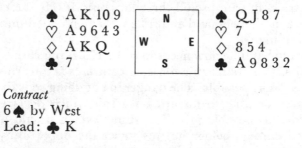

```
    ♠ A K 10 9              ♠ Q J 8 7
    ♡ A 9 6 4 3            ♡ 7
    ◇ A K Q               ◇ 8 5 4
    ♣ 7                   ♣ A 9 8 3 2
```

*Contract*
6♠ by West
Lead: ♣ K

To cash all three Diamonds here would be most dangerous. The seven-nil break of Clubs which might have affected the previous hand is less than a 1 per cent chance; a five-two break in Diamonds is as much as 31 per cent. In match-play such a mistake, while perhaps producing a gain of 100 points, might well lose 2,100. Hardly attractive. So we cash only two Diamonds and then cross-ruff to make eight trumps and four outside tops.

**Dummy reversal**

```
    ♠ none                 ♠ 10 8 6 5 4
    ♡ A Q 9 6 5           ♡ K J 10
    ◇ 8 5 2               ◇ A 7
    ♣ K Q J 4 2           ♣ A 10 8
```

*Contract*
7 ♡ by West
Lead: ♠ A

West has eleven tricks on top. He cannot trump Diamonds in dummy because he would first have to lose one, and even then he could trump only one and that's not enough. So the only possible play is to trump Spades in his own hand, turning the long- into the short-trump hand. This reduces his winning trumps to three, his winners on top to nine, so he needs to trump four times to reach his contract of thirteen.

The opening lead is trumped, dummy is entered first with the two Club entries, A and 10, and then with the ◇ A, each time ruffing back a Spade, leaving West with only one trump, not the ace—that should have been unblocked quickly—and this last trump passes the lead to dummy who plays off two more. On these last two trumps West discards his losing Diamonds, then takes the rest of the tricks with Clubs.

The play requires that the adverse trumps break 3–2 (68 per cent) and that nobody does any over-ruffing. A small extra chance in Spades makes the contract a 45 per cent chance. We have been in worse; and gone down in contracts twice as good.

The Club entries are used before the ◇ A because of the danger that one of the defenders could discard a Club on Spades to enable him to ruff the second Club, something which is much more probable than his being able to get rid of all his Diamonds.

## Ruffing finesse

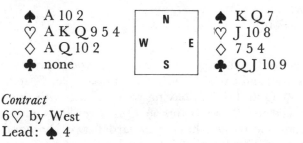

♠ A 10 2
♡ A K Q 9 5 4
◇ A Q 10 2
♣ none

♠ K Q 7
♡ J 10 8
◇ 7 5 4
♣ Q J 10 9

*Contract*
6 ♡ by West
Lead: ♠ 4

West takes Trick 1 in hand. His plan is clear and he needs to preserve the entries in dummy. He draws trumps ending in dummy, plays the ♣ Q and runs it to North's king, himself discarding a Diamond. North exits with a Spade. West plays dummy's ♣ J and runs it, discarding another Diamond. It wins. So the ten follows, South covering, West ruffing, and the Spade queen remains on the table as entry to enable West to discard his ◇ Q on the ♣ 9.

This particular hand can hardly be played any other way. The moment we see the opening lead of a Spade we appreciate that if North is superhuman enough to hold both top Clubs and fail to play one of them at Trick 1 against a slam, it would be ungenerous of us not to let him make both.

**Entry creation**

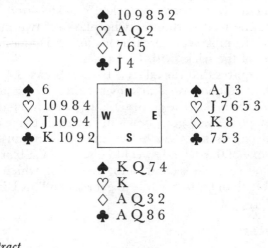

```
            ♠ 10 9 8 5 2
            ♡ A Q 2
            ◇ 7 6 5
            ♣ J 4
♠ 6                          ♠ A J 3
♡ 10 9 8 4      N            ♡ J 7 6 5 3
◇ J 10 9 4   W     E         ◇ K 8
♣ K 10 9 2      S            ♣ 7 5 3
            ♠ K Q 7 4
            ♡ K
            ◇ A Q 3 2
            ♣ A Q 8 6
```

*Contract*
4♠ by South
Lead: ◇ J

South really needs to be able to play trumps twice from dummy. The rest of the hand can somehow almost take care of itself. The play is the ♣ Q at Trick 3, having won Trick 1 with the ◇ Q and unblocked the ♡ K. If this ♣ Q is taken the knave is an entry to play one trump, having discarded two Diamonds on the top Hearts. The fourth Club can be ruffed high and the only possible losers are one Club and two trumps. In practice eleven tricks are made.

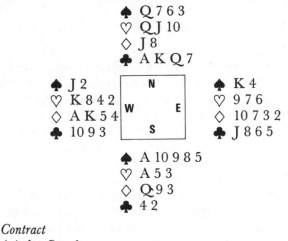

**♠** Q 7 6 3
**♡** Q J 10
**◇** J 8
**♣** A K Q 7

**♠** J 2
**♡** K 8 4 2
**◇** A K 5 4
**♣** 10 9 3

**♠** K 4
**♡** 9 7 6
**◇** 10 7 3 2
**♣** J 8 6 5

**♠** A 10 9 8 5
**♡** A 5 3
**◇** Q 9 3
**♣** 4 2

*Contract*
4 **♠** by South
Lead: ◇ A

West continued with two more rounds of Diamonds while South did not bother to make a trick with his queen, but ruffed it on the table. His concern was to lose one trump but no trick in Hearts. West if possible must be made to lead Hearts. The **♠** Q came from dummy, covered and won. South now played three top Clubs, throwing a Heart from hand and trumped the fourth round. If West had only one trump left he was inevitably end-played. Even if he didn't ruff he would be thrown-in with a trump at the next trick and be forced to give the contract.

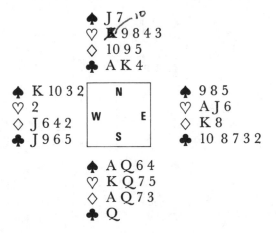

**♠** J 7 10
**♡** K 9 8 4 3
**◇** 10 9 5
**♣** A K 4

**♠** K 10 3 2
**♡** 2
**◇** J 6 4 2
**♣** J 9 6 5

**♠** 9 8 5
**♡** A J 6
**◇** K 8
**♣** 10 8 7 3 2

**♠** A Q 6 4
**♡** K Q 7 5
**◇** A Q 7 3
**♣** Q

*Contract*
4♡ by South
Lead: ◇ 2

From a National event this hand was played usually by South but at a few tables by North. The declarers sitting North, against the lead of the ♠ 9, had no trouble in wrapping up eleven tricks but those sitting South produced less happy results overall. Once we get a Diamond lead our objective should be to avoid two losers in trumps in case the Spade finesse should be wrong. To best attempt this we need entries in dummy so the plan should be to discard two Diamonds on top Clubs and to lead trumps twice from dummy, the available entries being the ♠ J and a Spade ruff. At Trick 2 therefore the ♣ Q is unblocked and followed by the ♠ Q. If this is ducked the hand can be played on a cross-ruff to concede two tricks in trumps and nothing else. If taken, we have the necessary two entries and again can produce eleven tricks, leading trumps twice from dummy.

Several players of reputation actually went down here, playing the trump king at Trick 2. East took this and returned the ◇ 8 causing the declarer frequently to panic into the belief that a Diamond ruff threatened—as in a way it did—and to play the ♡ Q, hoping to drop the knave. They had now left themselves with blocked Hearts, untouched Clubs and a loser in Diamonds emerging from almost nowhere. Seldom was a hand so massacred, yet the plan at Trick 1 makes the play simple and logical.

*And:*

```
                  ♠ A K Q
                  ♡ 4 3 2
                  ◇ A 7
                  ♣ J 8 6 4 3
      ♠ 4              N           ♠ 10 9 7 6 3
      ♡ 10 9 7 5                   ♡ 6
      ◇ J 6 3      W     E         ◇ K 10 8 5 4 2
      ♣ A K Q 9 5      S           ♣ 2
                  ♠ J 8 5 2
                  ♡ A K Q J 8
                  ◇ Q 9
                  ♣ 10 7
```

*Contract*
4♡ by South
Lead: ♣ A
(W–E game)

West cashed two rounds of Clubs and then played a small one, East ruffing, South over-ruffing with the 8. He now drew trumps, expecting to make five tricks in Hearts, four in Spades and one Diamond. But four trumps in one hand against him meant that Spades were inescapably blocked. The answer however was simple enough. West had said nothing during the bidding so could hardly hold the ◇ K as well as that Club suit. East was out of Clubs and Hearts so all should be well. On the fourth round of trumps therefore South discarded the Diamond ace, cashed the top Spades and played the ◇ 7 from dummy, his last three cards being the ♠ J and ◇ Q 9. East took his ◇ K but could do no more.

South was slightly fortunate here in that East held no trump higher than that 6. Had he held West's 9 that would have cost South a picture to over-ruff and automatically promoted West's ten. Please check this analysis.

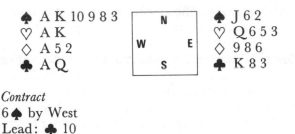

♠ A K 10 9 8 3    N    ♠ J 6 2
♡ A K                   ♡ Q 6 5 3
◇ A 5 2          W   E   ◇ 9 8 6
♣ A Q                S    ♣ K 8 3

*Contract*
6♠ by West
Lead: ♣ 10

West wins the Club lead and should do so with the ace, not for any particular reason at the moment but because he is over-loaded with entries while dummy has few. Examining the hand however he appreciates that while he can cash two top Hearts and, finding an entry to dummy, discard something on the ♡ Q, this still leaves him with one losing Diamond and dependent upon losing no trick in trumps. The ♣ Q therefore must be unblocked, not overtaken, and the ♣ K used to jettison the second Diamond loser.

The play at Trick 2 is consequently the ♠ 10, conceding a

trick to the ♠ Q and using the ♠ J as the entry. This must be taken by the defence unless one player is void. If so, and the ten is refused, the two Hearts and the ♣ Q are cashed and if North has the trumps a small card is led towards the knave, ensuring an entry. If South has the trumps West can play most safely by overtaking the ♣ Q and employing a trump finesse after cashing the ♡ Q. Or by playing the ♠ 9 or 8 and overtaking when the ♠ 6 will provide the necessary entry. West's ♠ 3 must be carefully preserved for that possible situation.

## Seven-card trump-suit

|  |  |  |
|---|---|---|
| ♠ 5 | **N** | ♠ J 4 2 |
| ♡ A K Q 10 | **W    E** | ♡ J 5 4 |
| ◇ A 7 3 | **S** | ◇ J 8 6 4 2 |
| ♣ A K 10 8 4 |  | ♣ Q J |

*Contract*
4♡ by West
Lead: ♠ A

A good contract to reach. The defence attacked with top Spades but West, conscious that a 4–2 break of trumps was more likely than 3–3 (48 per cent against 36 per cent; four times from seven), refused to shorten his holding, instead discarding two small Diamonds at Tricks 2 and 3, cards which were likely to be losers anyway. Taking the next trick he drew trumps—and 4–2 they were—and made his contract comfortably with four Hearts, one Diamond and five Clubs. This is standard technique in such circumstances.

This takes us back to the hand before last where we needed to check the analysis. South there played well by unblocking his ◇ A, but was he really lucky that East held no trump high enough to force a picture from him—as of course West had hoped when playing the third Club? For he actually had no need whatever to over-ruff. He had a loser in the ◇ Q which he could discard with perfect safety. So, looking further, why over-ruff that miserable little six? Why not preserve his trump *length*? Once he appreciates that, the hand presents no further problem. *But here:*

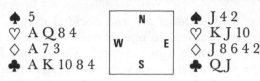

♠ 5  
♡ A Q 8 4  
◇ A 7 3  
♣ A K 10 8 4

♠ J 4 2  
♡ K J 10  
◇ J 8 6 4 2  
♣ Q J

*Contract*  
4 ♡ by West  
Lead: ♠ A

we should analyse deeper.

West-East with similar hands reach the same contract and are opposed by the same defence. There is, however, one important difference, the trumps being split differently, those in dummy not capable of being over-ruffed. Now, while to discard two Diamonds may cope with a 4–2 break of trumps, we may actually be able to cope with a 5–1 break. This we could not do with the last hand. And, as that break is a 15 per cent chance, it is worth looking at. There are three tops outside trumps so to succeed we need seven tricks more. Four with West should be easy enough; the second and third rounds of Spades may be ruffed small so, if we can ruff three Clubs in dummy, that's enough.

This hand is one where the experienced player may easily go wrong. The pattern of seven trumps allied to comfortable discards which will preserve his length is so familiar that he sometimes fails to look deeper.

So the second Spade is ruffed, two top Clubs played and another ruffed, ruff third Spade, another Club, back via the ◇ A to ruff the third Club and we have eight tricks while the A Q of Hearts remain to take the other two.

## Losing control

♠ Q J 10 4  
♡ 7 5  
◇ A 5 4  
♣ A 8 6 2

♠ K 7 3  
♡ Q J 10  
◇ K Q 9 8 2  
♣ K 5

*Contract*  
4 ♠ by West  
Lead: ♣ Q

West won the lead with his ace and decided that he ought to establish a trick in Hearts, so played one. South won and continued Clubs, dummy's king winning while West felt fairly comfortable, returning to hand with the ◇ A to play another Heart, North taking the ace and playing another Club. At this stage the hand blew up with South over-ruffing while North sat with A 9 to four trumps.

With this type of close run hand we have no time to bother with possible bad breaks. If somebody stops the Diamonds or holds five trumps, that's just too bad. We must play on reasonable breaks, the odds on our side. Trumps therefore at Trick 2, take the second Club and draw all the trumps, relying on Diamonds, thus making five Diamonds, two Clubs and three trumps.

## Two become one

```
                    ♠ A 8 6
                    ♡ 8 7 4
                    ◇ Q J 9
                    ♣ A Q J 2
  ♠ Q J 10 5    ┌─────────────┐   ♠ K 9 7 3
  ♡ A          │      N      │   ♡ K 5
  ◇ 10 8 6 4 3 │ W         E │   ◇ A 7 5 2
  ♣ 9 6 3      │      S      │   ♣ 10 8 5
               └─────────────┘
                    ♠ 4 2
                    ♡ Q J 10 9 6 3 2
                    ◇ K
                    ♣ K 7 4
```

*Contract*
4 ♡ by South
Lead: ♠ Q

A nice easy contract if only they had found any other lead; now however with four losers on top. Clearly if the defence is permitted to gain the lead before one of those losers has been eliminated the contract will fail. So, as the only suit we can play while retaining the lead is Clubs, Clubs we must play. Four rounds, discarding a Spade or a Diamond on the fourth,

immaterial which and also immaterial what East does about it.
If he ruffs, the two top trumps will fall together; if he refuses to
ruff West will either ruff with his ace of trumps or let that Club
win. Once Clubs are 3–3 there is no defence unless one defender
holds all three outstanding trumps. *or they are divided  A K / x*

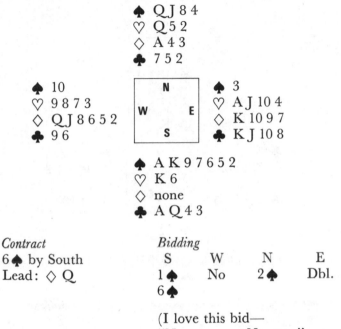

```
              ♠ Q J 8 4
              ♡ Q 5 2
              ◇ A 4 3
              ♣ 7 5 2

♠ 10                          ♠ 3
♡ 9 8 7 3          N          ♡ A J 10 4
◇ Q J 8 6 5 2   W     E       ◇ K 10 9 7
♣ 9 6              S          ♣ K J 10 8

              ♠ A K 9 7 6 5 2
              ♡ K 6
              ◇ none
              ♣ A Q 4 3
```

| Contract | Bidding | | | |
|----------|---------|---|---|---|
| 6 ♠ by South | S | W | N | E |
| Lead: ◇ Q | 1 ♠ | No | 2 ♠ | Dbl. |
|  | 6 ♠ | | | |

(I love this bid—
"No-nonsense Norman"
they call me!)

*muddled up analysis*

The key here is to refrain from playing the ◇ A at Trick 1 but
rather preserve it until we have some idea about what we should
discard on it. Ruff. Draw trumps ending in dummy. Play a
~~Club~~. If East wins, dummy has two discards for us while the
Spade finesse is surely right on the bidding. If he plays low our
king wins, dummy is entered and ~~that king~~ discarded on the
*the heart* preserved ◇ A.

# Thinking It Out

**Defence**

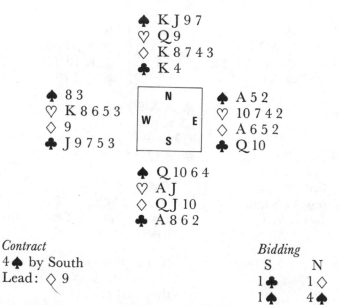

```
              ♠ K J 9 7
              ♡ Q 9
              ◇ K 8 7 4 3
              ♣ K 4

♠ 8 3              N              ♠ A 5 2
♡ K 8 6 5 3    W      E          ♡ 10 7 4 2
◇ 9                              ◇ A 6 5 2
♣ J 9 7 5 3        S             ♣ Q 10

              ♠ Q 10 6 4
              ♡ A J
              ◇ Q J 10
              ♣ A 8 6 2
```

*Contract*
4♠ by South
Lead: ◇ 9

*Bidding*

| S | N |
|---|---|
| 1♣ | 1◇ |
| 1♠ | 4♠ |

East wins Trick 1 with his ace and considers whether to give his partner an immediate ruff. The lead is an obvious singleton; the only other cards missing are Q J 10 which makes any other type of lead out of the question. It also marks South as being short in Hearts. If he has five cards in Clubs he must have the ♡ A single for have it he must for his opening bid. Next, West almost certainly has two trumps but cannot have more, so one ruff is the maximum possible. If however he is given it at once there will be discards on dummy's Diamonds if required and any Heart loser will no longer be lost. East therefore plays a Heart at Trick 2 and, when in with the ♠ A, gives West his Diamond ruff to defeat the hand.

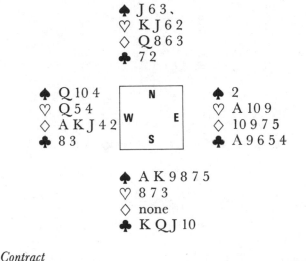

♠ J 6 3
♡ K J 6 2
◇ Q 8 6 3
♣ 7 2

♠ Q 10 4
♡ Q 5 4
◇ A K J 4 2
♣ 8 3

♠ 2
♡ A 10 9
◇ 10 9 7 5
♣ A 9 6 5 4

♠ A K 9 8 7 5
♡ 8 7 3
◇ none
♣ K Q J 10

*Contract*
4♠ by South
Lead: ◇ A

South ruffed at Trick 1 and played the Club king. On the lead the Heart ace was likely to be with East and maybe the queen as well. But he needed the queen to be on his left unless the ♠ Q came down. East ducked. South played the queen and East won, noting that West had petered to show a doubleton.

That pretty well exposed South's hand—six trumps, four Clubs, no Diamonds; so room for three small Hearts. If trumps were solid there was nothing to be done for only two tricks in Hearts could be taken. And, as it had become clear that South now held two good Clubs the Heart harvest might well be reduced to one—unless declarer's secondary control was swiftly removed. East realised that this was the only chance so played the ♡ 10. South cashed two trumps but the queen failed to drop. He switched to Clubs. If he could get one Heart away successfully he was home for it did not matter if the last Club was ruffed or not. East would be on play with the ♡ A but void of Spades. South's third Heart could be trumped.

West did not wait; the trump queen went on the first Club and a Heart through dummy's king to East's tenace defeated the hand.

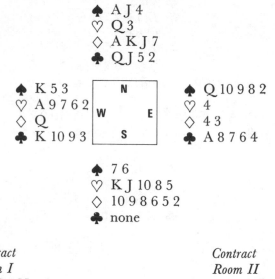

♠ A J 4
♡ Q 3
◇ A K J 7
♣ Q J 5 2

♠ K 5 3
♡ A 9 7 6 2
◇ Q
♣ K 10 9 3

♠ Q 10 9 8 2
♡ 4
◇ 4 3
♣ A 8 7 6 4

♠ 7 6
♡ K J 10 8 5
◇ 10 9 8 6 5 2
♣ none

| Contract<br>Room I<br>5◇ by North<br>Lead: ♡ 4 | Contract<br>Room II<br>4♡ by South<br>Lead: ◇ Q |
|---|---|

In Room I, 5◇ by North, East took his ruff in Hearts at Trick 2 but that was the end. North drew trumps in one round, ruffed all his Clubs in dummy and threw two Spades on good Hearts. To this contract there was no defence.

In Room II, 4♡, South played trumps at Trick 2 and West correctly took the second round. He now led a small Club to East's ace, South throwing a Spade. East gave West his Diamond ruff but now South had three trumps to West's two and could ruff, draw and cash.

The lead of shortage in order to obtain an early ruff is often the best defence but trump holdings must have some bearing on decision. Holding queen to three, the lead of a singleton is unlikely to benefit the defence even if a ruff is obtained. King and another is hardly recommended but is a better holding than queen to three for there is still a chance that declarer may⁻ finesse. Length however is the primary factor, especially when primary support lacks. Primary trump-support of four cards inevitably means that one hand can take ruffs without affecting the basic trump-length for declarer. With only secondary support the matter is quite different. If the long trump hand can be made to ruff a couple of times a defender with a four-card holding in trumps may well be in a position to snatch trump control.

In this hand East was reasonable in leading his singleton but West cannot be too strongly criticised for leading his. He should have led from length, a Club seems right but a Spade would have been just as effective. Once that Spade ace has gone and the second round of trumps is taken, the defence gets the hand down anything from two to four tricks according to how declarer tackles it.

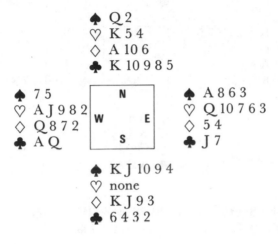

```
                 ♠ Q 2
                 ♡ K 5 4
                 ◇ A 10 6
                 ♣ K 10 9 8 5

   ♠ 7 5            N            ♠ A 8 6 3
   ♡ A J 9 8 2                   ♡ Q 10 7 6 3
   ◇ Q 8 7 2    W       E        ◇ 5 4
   ♣ A Q            S            ♣ J 7

                 ♠ K J 10 9 4
                 ♡ none
                 ◇ K J 9 3
                 ♣ 6 4 3 2
```

*Contract*
4 ♠ by South
Lead: ♡ A

South ruffed the opening lead and played a Club. West took his ace and, psychologically shattered by the ruff of his ace to say nothing of the situation of his ♣ Q, switched to Diamonds, unaware but not blissfully that he had found the only lead to break the contract. South now romped home in a situation where it should have been impossible.

A Heart continuation, removing dummy's control of the suit, leaves South wide open to the forcing game. East merely takes the second round of trumps and continues Hearts, reducing South to one trump while he himself has two—and two more

Hearts as well. The contract inevitably goes two down. Timing is all-important of course. Should East hold up his trump ace until the third round—there won't be a third round. South will switch to Clubs, content to lose two trumps and the Club ace.

## Thinking it through

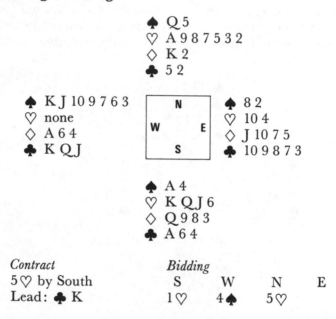

```
                    ♠ Q 5
                    ♡ A 9 8 7 5 3 2
                    ◇ K 2
                    ♣ 5 2

♠ K J 10 9 7 6 3         N          ♠ 8 2
♡ none                              ♡ 10 4
◇ A 6 4          W          E       ◇ J 10 7 5
♣ K Q J                 S          ♣ 10 9 8 7 3

                    ♠ A 4
                    ♡ K Q J 6
                    ◇ Q 9 8 3
                    ♣ A 6 4
```

| *Contract* | *Bidding* | | | |
|---|---|---|---|---|
| 5♡ by South | S | W | N | E |
| Lead: ♣ K | 1♡ | 4♠ | 5♡ | |

South took the second Club, ruffed one, drew trumps, ending in his own hand and then played a Diamond, dummy's king winning. He now considered that he had a good end-play in the middle. If West held either knave or ten of Diamonds, a finesse of the eight would force him either to return the suit away from his ace or play away from his ♠ K. A Diamond would enable South to establish his queen and on it discard dummy's losing Spade.

East however held both minor honours and inserted the ten. South covered, fearing to let it hold lest a Spade come through. West won and returned the suit. Dummy ruffed but the knave did not fall and South was left with an inescapable Spade loser.

This was a good example of muddled thinking plus a lack of thinking in depth. The bidding had practically guaranteed a seven-card suit of Spades. With only six, giving West four Diamonds to the ace, no longer a single-suited hand, the bid would surely have been either 2 ♠ or Double—even with a slight stretch, 2 ♡. So South put West on play with a Diamond—or rather, intended to—to force him to play away from his ace. When the ten came he suddenly decided to play West for a four-card suit in Diamonds. The simpler way would have been to play small on the ten, take his Spade ace and then ruff out the ◇ A, by then surely dropping.

But overall a complete end-play was there if South had thought the hand through. Dummy plays off all the trumps to leave:

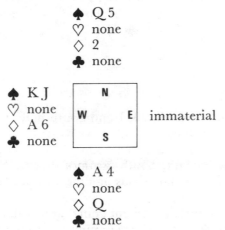

```
              ♠ Q 5
              ♡ none
              ◇ 2
              ♣ none

  ♠ K J                       N
  ♡ none                 W         E     immaterial
  ◇ A 6                       S
  ♣ none

              ♠ A 4
              ♡ none
              ◇ Q
              ♣ none
```

West with four cards, has still to play to the last trump and is wondering whether to blank his Spade king to be dropped or his ◇ A to be thrown-in with it. In all such situations declarers should visualize the remaining few cards if the last trump is played. This will frequently lead to a successful choice of play.

## More immediate thinking

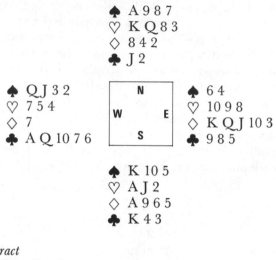

                    ♠ A 9 8 7
                    ♡ K Q 8 3
                    ◇ 8 4 2
                    ♣ J 2

    ♠ Q J 3 2                      ♠ 6 4
    ♡ 7 5 4          N             ♡ 10 9 8
    ◇ 7          W       E         ◇ K Q J 10 3
    ♣ A Q 10 7 6        S          ♣ 9 8 5

                    ♠ K 10 5
                    ♡ A J 2
                    ◇ A 9 6 5
                    ♣ K 4 3

*Contract*
3 NT by South
Lead: ♣ 7

The Club knave wins Trick 1 and South notes that East drops
the ♣ 5. As South can see all lower cards this is East's lowest,
and again, as East didn't start a low peter to show that he held
four cards in the suit, South assumes that he hasn't got four
which gives West a dangerous holding with an initial five-card
suit.

Well, something must be got going, and without letting East
on lead, so the ♠ 7 comes from dummy, South playing the ♠ 10,
unblocking in fact for if at some later stage East can be counted
for two Spades only, to retain the 10 would block the suit and
prevent the finesse which can be made if South has the ♠ 5
instead. West wins and switches to a Heart.

South takes the Heart in hand and cashes his second winner
in the suit. He sees the ♡ 9 drop of this second round, which
suggests that the suit is breaking evenly. He plays off the
remaining two in dummy, discarding a Diamond. East discards
a Club, West the ◇ 7.

Now if Spades broke evenly the contract was safe with four
Hearts, three Spades, one Club and one Diamond. If East held

four the contract was likely to fail. If West had the four he
started with five Clubs, four Spades, three Hearts and one
Diamond—just discarded. On the other hand if West held only
two Spades he started with three Diamonds and is now down to
two. Surely not queen doubleton—he could have thrown his
last Spade. King doubleton perhaps? Then an end-play is
possible unless he unblocks the king on the ace. South plays the
Diamond ace and the hand is exposed. He plays his ♠ K and
takes the finesse he had prepared at Trick 2. And that of course
was a mistake. He should have catered for every possible type of
false-carding by the defence, maybe something new in his
experience, but immaterial now; he should have won the third
Spade with the ace and end-played West with the fourth,
forcing him to lead Clubs to South's king. The contract was
made, but the technique fell just short of perfection.

**Thin ice**

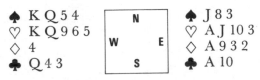

♠ K Q 5 4
♡ K Q 9 6 5
◇ 4
♣ Q 4 3

N
W E
S

♠ J 8 3
♡ A J 10 3
◇ A 9 3 2
♣ A 10

*Contract*
6♡ by West
Lead: ◇ K

This is a messy slam, thin ice indeed, so we must play it as safely
as we can. Obviously we need the trumps to be split evenly
because we have to ruff two Clubs in dummy after discarding
one on the fourth round of Spades. On the way to doing that we
must try to ensure that we actually have a winning fourth round
of that suit.

Dummy looks to be full of entries. Actually it is extremely
short of them. We play one round of trumps, the ace, and then
a small Spade to the king. It wins. Dummy is re-entered with
another trump and another small Spade is played towards the
queen. This caters for either a three–three break or for South to
hold the doubleton ace. We cannot cater for North to have that
as it would mean winning first with the knave and then ducking
the second round, a procedure which causes us to lose two tricks

in the suit if they break evenly. (And would make us look extremely foolish as well.) South takes the ace and plays a Diamond. The Spade knave is unblocked after ruffing this and another Diamond ruff enables us to discard that ♣ 10 on the fourth Spade. The remaining small cards are cross-ruffed without trouble.

Indeed a messy slam. Even by the most generous allowances in simple point-count we can't scrape up more than 29 points. But sometimes we reach these contracts. Accurate play will enable us to make quite a few.

**Bread-and-butter stuff: make your plan**

1
| ♠ A Q 9 4 2 | N | ♠ K 6 5 3 |
| ♡ 5 2 | W    E | ♡ 10 6 3 |
| ◇ A Q 7 | S | ◇ K 8 4 |
| ♣ A K 8 | | ♣ 7 5 2 |

*Hand 1.* West plays 4♠. The attack is three rounds of Hearts.

2
| ♠ A Q J 9 4 2 | N | ♠ K 10 8 5 3 |
| ♡ A Q 6 | W    E | ♡ 7 5 3 |
| ◇ A | S | ◇ J 7 |
| ♣ A Q 2 | | ♣ K 5 4 |

*Hand 2.* West plays 6♠. *Lead:* ◇ K.

3
| ♠ 8 5 3 | N | ♠ J 4 2 |
| ♡ A K J 9 7 | W    E | ♡ Q 8 2 |
| ◇ Q 8 | S | ◇ A K 5 4 2 |
| ♣ A 8 3 | | ♣ 7 5 |

*Hand 3.* West plays 4♡. North cashes three Spades, then plays a Club.

4
| ♠ 8 2 | N | ♠ A 7 6 5 4 |
| ♡ 5 3 | W    E | ♡ A K 6 2 |
| ◇ K J 9 2 | S | ◇ A 5 |
| ♣ K J 9 6 4 | | ♣ Q 10 |

*Hand 4.* West plays 3 NT. *Lead:* ◇ 3.

*Hand 1.* The third Heart is trumped and dummy is entered with the ♠ K, preserving two tops with West to guard against a void with North. If this obtains, the double finesse is exposed, the first taken at once while the ◇ K is the entry for the second.

*Hand 2.* Placing North with the ◇ Q on his lead, West plans to end-play him. Trumps are drawn and Clubs eliminated, ending in dummy. The ◇ J is led and the ♡ 6 discarded. North, on play, must either lead into the ♡ A Q or concede a ruff-and-discard.

*Hand 3.* The ♣ A is taken and two rounds of trumps follow, leaving the queen in dummy. If they break 3–2, two rounds of Diamonds plus a ruff of a small one (with a high trump) should establish an extra trick against the normal 4–2 break and the ♡ Q remains as entry, simultaneously drawing the last trump. If trumps break 4–1 they are all drawn, the ◇ Q being the entry to return to West's hand and he has to rely on a 3–3 break in Diamonds.

*Hand 4.* The ◇ A must be taken at Trick 1, the extra trick that is provided by the lead into the king-knave tenace being declined. Clubs are then established, overtaking the second round if necessary in order to clear the suit. Nine tricks are now available with only two in Diamonds. To let the lead run to the tenace permits the defence to take the second Club, cutting communication and then playing entirely on the dummy.

| 5 | ♠ A Q 4<br>♡ A J 7 2<br>◇ 4 3<br>♣ A 9 8 6 | N<br>W    E<br>S | ♠ 8<br>♡ 8 4<br>◇ A K J 8 6 5 2<br>♣ J 5 3 |

*Hand 5.* West plays 3 NT. *Lead:* ♠ 5.

| 6 | ♠ Q J 4<br>♡ A J 4<br>◇ A Q 2<br>♣ A J 9 3 | N<br>W    E<br>S | ♠ A 10 9 5<br>♡ 10 5 2<br>◇ 6 5<br>♣ Q 10 8 5 |

*Hand 6.* West plays 3 NT. *Lead:* ◇ 4.

| 7 | ♠ A Q J 6 2<br>♡ A 8 6 3<br>◇ K 5<br>♣ A 4 | N<br>W    E<br>S | ♠ 8 5 4<br>♡ K 7 4<br>◇ A Q J 10 2<br>♣ K 6 |

*Hand 7.* West plays 6♠. *Lead:* ♣ Q.

8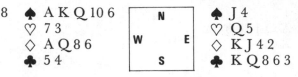

     ♠ A K Q 10 6               ♠ J 4
     ♡ 7 3                     ♡ Q 5
     ◇ A Q 8 6             ◇ K J 4 2
     ♣ 5 4                   ♣ K Q 8 6 3

*Hand 8.* West plays 4♠. South wins Trick 1 with the ♡ A and switches to a trump.

*Hand 5.* At Trick 2 a Diamond must be played and, if North play the ◇ 7, the ◇ 8 is finessed. If North plays a higher card it must be ducked. The danger is that South could be void when the finesse of the ◇ J reduces six tricks to three.

*Hand 6.* At Trick 2 the ♣ A must be played, followed by a small one to concede the king. The second round of Diamonds may then be ducked to cut communications and the Spade finesse taken later into the safe hand.

*Hand 7.* The danger here is a four–one trump split. We need to play the ace first to guard against a singleton being the king with North. Then trumps must be played twice from dummy to cater for South having king to four. Thus the ♣ A must be taken at Trick 1 to preserve the entries in dummy.

*Hand 8.* Trick 2 must be taken by the knave to guard against five trumps in one hand and dummy being forced by a third round of Hearts when the defence obtains the lead with the ♣ A. One Club trick is the tenth. The ♣ K should therefore be played at Trick 3 and the contract is now safe.

9

    ♠ A 8 4               ♠ 7 2
    ♡ A J                 ♡ K Q 10 5
    ◇ Q 10 8 6         ◇ A 7
    ♣ K J 7 3          ♣ Q 10 8 6 5

*Hand 9.* West plays 3 NT. *Lead:* ◇ 2.

10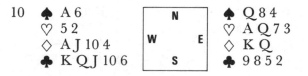

    ♠ A 6                 ♠ Q 8 4
    ♡ 5 2                ♡ A Q 7 3
    ◇ A J 10 4          ◇ K Q
    ♣ K Q J 10 6       ♣ 9 8 5 2

*Hand 10.* West plays 5♣. *Lead:* ♡ 2.

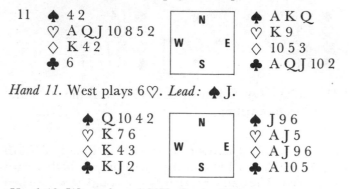

11    ♠ 4 2
      ♡ A Q J 10 8 5 2
      ◇ K 4 2
      ♣ 6

      ♠ A K Q
      ♡ K 9
      ◇ 10 5 3
      ♣ A Q J 10 2

*Hand 11.* West plays 6♡. *Lead:* ♠ J.

      ♠ Q 10 4 2
      ♡ K 7 6
      ◇ K 4 3
      ♣ K J 2

      ♠ J 9 6
      ♡ A J 5
      ◇ A J 9 6
      ♣ A 10 5

*Hand 12.* West plays 3 NT. *Lead:* ♡ 4.

*Hand 9.* We are fortunate here not to get a Spade lead. The risk must not be taken that South may have the ◇ K, win and switch to Spades. The ◇ A must be played and then Clubs established immediately.

*Hand 10.* The ♡ K may be with North but we cannot risk that. The ♡ A must be played at Trick 1 and then the trumps cleared. Unless there are four in one hand we are then safe. Diamonds will take care of East's losing Spades and one Spade ruff is enough, making four Clubs, one ruff, four Diamonds and the two major aces.

*Hand 11.* Play ♣ A at Trick 2, ruff a Club with the ace, play small trump to dummy's nine and ruff another Club, a trump to the king and ruff another Club, draw trumps if necessary. If the ♣ K has not fallen, being to five, enter dummy, throw one Diamond on the third Spade and play South for the ◇ A.

*Hand 12.* Take Trick 1 with the ♡ K. Attack Spades. The Heart finesse is taken on the second round. It may lose but South will have no more unless the suit breaks 4–3. To play the knave at Trick 1 and find South with a doubleton queen could be fatal.

13    ♠ Q J 4 2
      ♡ A Q 5
      ◇ K 7
      ♣ Q 10 9 4

      ♠ K 10 8
      ♡ 7 4
      ◇ A J 5 2
      ♣ A J 8 6

*Hand 13.* West plays 3 NT. *Lead:* ♡ 6.

14    ♠ A 10 8 6 5 2     [N / W E / S]     ♠ Q 4 3
        ♡ A Q 3                         ♡ 7 5
        ◇ A 2                           ◇ K Q J 4
        ♣ 8 6                           ♣ K Q J 3

*Hand 14.* West plays 6♠. North leads the ♣ A and then a Heart.

15    ♠ A Q 6 5 4     [N / W E / S]     ♠ K J 10
        ♡ J 5 3                       ♡ A 10 9 8 4 2
        ◇ A Q 4 2                   ◇ 6
        ♣ 9                           ♣ A K Q

*Hand 15.* West plays 7♠. *Lead:* ♣ 8.

16    ♠ A J 4     [N / W E / S]     ♠ Q 9 7 5 2
        ♡ J 10 9                      ♡ A 8 7
        ◇ A K Q 9 7 6             ◇ 10 5 3
        ♣ 8                           ♣ A 3

*Hand 16.* West plays 5◇. *Lead:* ♣ K. (Trumps are 2–2.)

*Hand 13.* Spades must be attacked at once. The second Heart is ducked to cut communications. The Club finesse can be taken later into the safe hand.

*Hand 14.* The only hope here is to find the singleton knave of trumps with North. A singleton king does not help. The queen is played from dummy, hoping to force the king, pin the knave. Dummy's last entry then just suffices to enable us to take the finesse of the ♠ 8 against nine and another with South.

*Hand 15.* We must play on a 3–2 break in trumps which is good provided nobody is void of Hearts. Play three rounds of Clubs, discarding two Hearts. Then ♡ A and a Heart ruffed with the ♠ A. Enter dummy with a trump and ruff another Heart with the ♠ Q. Draw trumps in dummy.

*Hand 16.* Take the ♣ A and ruff the small Club at once. Draw trumps and play the ace knave of Spades. The Spade situation is revealed and to avoid giving the contract at once whoever wins the ♠ K must play a Heart. If North plays it, it is run and South, winning, is end-played. If South wins the ♠ K a Heart from him kills North's honour.

# Coup

**Two coups**

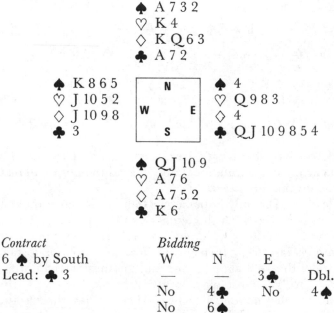

```
                    ♠ A 7 3 2
                    ♡ K 4
                    ◇ K Q 6 3
                    ♣ A 7 2
    ♠ K 8 6 5                        ♠ 4
    ♡ J 10 5 2                       ♡ Q 9 8 3
    ◇ J 10 9 8                       ◇ 4
    ♣ 3                              ♣ Q J 10 9 8 5 4
                    ♠ Q J 10 9
                    ♡ A 7 6
                    ◇ A 7 5 2
                    ♣ K 6
```

| Contract | Bidding | | | |
|---|---|---|---|---|
| 6 ♠ by South | W | N | E | S |
| Lead: ♣ 3 | — | — | 3♣ | Dbl. |
| | No | 4♣ | No | 4♠ |
| | No | 6♠ | | |

South won in hand and took the finesse in trumps twice, the bad break exposed. This was not too serious—the hand was reasonable enough to make a grand slam on that finesse. Nevertheless care might be needed because West could well stop the Diamonds, marked as he was with a singleton Club. So the ace of Clubs had better make a trick, which meant playing towards it. No danger that West would waste his trump on a small Club, leaving the ace there to provide a discard. South plays his Club, West discarding a Heart, dummy winning.

Next, king, ace and a Heart ruff, all following, which meant that West held at least three Diamonds, the only danger being that he might hold four. ◇ K therefore, then ◇ A, East showing out and the count complete, East 7–4–1–1, West 4–4–4–1. The only hope now was a smother play the technique for which demanded that the lead be thrown at Trick 11 to *East*.

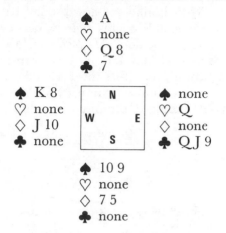

```
              ♠ A
              ♡ none
              ◇ Q 8
              ♣ 7
  ♠ K 8                      ♠ none
  ♡ none     N              ♡ Q
  ◇ J 10   W     E          ◇ none
  ♣ none     S              ♣ Q J 9
              ♠ 10 9
              ♡ none
              ◇ 7 5
              ♣ none
```

A Diamond goes to the queen and dummy plays the Club, South discarding his losing Diamond. South ruffs whatever East plays and West is helpless.
*And:*

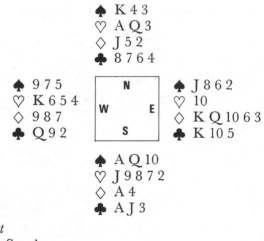

```
              ♠ K 4 3
              ♡ A Q 3
              ◇ J 5 2
              ♣ 8 7 6 4
  ♠ 9 7 5                    ♠ J 8 6 2
  ♡ K 6 5 4   N             ♡ 10
  ◇ 9 8 7   W     E         ◇ K Q 10 6 3
  ♣ Q 9 2     S             ♣ K 10 5
              ♠ A Q 10
              ♡ J 9 8 7 2
              ◇ A 4
              ♣ A J 3
```

*Contract*
4♡ by South
Lead: ◇ 9

The contract looks edgy. The defence has found a good lead so South must lose one Diamond, almost certainly two Clubs and maybe a trump as well. He takes Trick 1 and plays for a doubleton king of trumps on his left, finessing the queen. When the ten drops it looks like four to the king on his left, apparently a certain loser. It looks like one down unless he can produce a position. Both top Clubs on his right would do. If only one, maybe something can be done. He plays a Club, East following small, and "finesses" the knave. East wins and continues Diamonds, South ruffing the third round. The position is possible. South runs another trump, cashes his ♣ A and then plays off Spades, ending in dummy to produce:

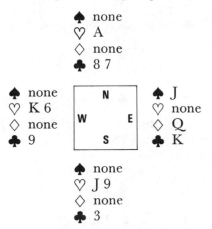

The Club comes from dummy, putting East on play. South trumps whatever he plays next and West may under-ruff and lose the last trick to the trump ace, or he may over-ruff, be over-ruffed and lose the last trick to the trump knave.

The "smother" technique does not apply uniquely to adverse kings; it moves with the target.

**N–S game**

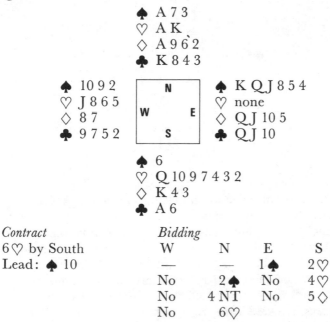

**Contract**
6♡ by South
Lead: ♠ 10

**Bidding**

| W | N | E | S |
|---|---|---|---|
| — | — | 1♠ | 2♡ |
| No | 2♠ | No | 4♡ |
| No | 4 NT | No | 5◊ |
| No | 6♡ | | |

South wins Trick 1 with dummy's ace and plays the ♡ A, learning the bad news at once. East has opened on one king and good shape, probably solidity also, but is unlikely to have a seven-card suit or his bid at this vulnerability would have more likely been 3♠. On the first lead he dropped the ♠ 8, a mild indication that he does not have the 9. This suggests that West started with 10 9 and another, so can guard against the ♠ 7 in dummy. That puts a squeeze over Spades and Diamonds out of court. East can throw all his Spades with impunity. Any other squeeze is out; East cannot hold four of both minor suits while, should South give up a trick in Hearts West would probably remove a vital menace and ruin any such idea.

Dummy however has plenty of cards which can be ruffed and South, counting them, realises that he might be able to reduce his trump-length to correspond with West's. At Trick 2 therefore South ruffs back a Spade, then plays two top Clubs and ruffs one, enters with the ◊ A and ruffs the last Spade. The position is now:

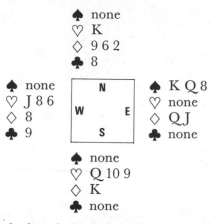

♠ none
♡ K
◇ 9 6 2
♣ 8

♠ none     ♠ K Q 8
♡ J 8 6    ♡ none
◇ 8        ◇ Q J
♣ 9        ♣ none

♠ none
♡ Q 10 9
◇ K
♣ none

The ◇ K is cashed and the losing Diamond played. If West discards, East wins and must play a Spade, ruffed by South with the ♡ 9. West cannot over-ruff for then he is in turn over-ruffed by dummy's king, leaving South's trumps good. If he under-ruffs the K Q of trumps take the last two tricks. He may ruff the losing Diamond himself and play a trump, but South merely ruffs back the last Club to which West must follow suit and takes Trick 13 with the ♡ Q.

We see that the technique moves with the target for here the throw-in comes at Trick 10 instead of, as with the king to be smothered, at Trick 11.

### Trump coup against right-hand opponent

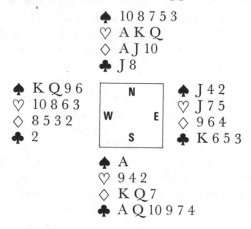

♠ 10 8 7 5 3
♡ A K Q
◇ A J 10
♣ J 8

♠ K Q 9 6     ♠ J 4 2
♡ 10 8 6 3    ♡ J 7 5
◇ 8 5 3 2     ◇ 9 6 4
♣ 2         ♣ K 6 5 3

♠ A
♡ 9 4 2
◇ K Q 7
♣ A Q 10 9 7 4

*Contract*
7♣ by South
Lead: ♠ K

The slam appears to hinge on the trump finesse but, taking Trick 1 with his blank ace, entering dummy with the ◇ 10 and taking two finesses in trumps, South finds that East still holds the guarded king. So the only hope is a trump reduction play; he must reduce his own trump-length to that of East and so arrange matters that dummy has to lead to Trick 12. What dummy leads is immaterial. South's last two cards must be the A Q of trumps, a tenace over East's king and another. South started with six trumps, East with four. Consequently he must ruff twice and still have an entry remaining in dummy for the final coup. Fortunately there are plenty.

Dummy is entered via the ◇ A and a Spade trumped, entered with the ♡ A and another Spade trumped. Now it becomes necessary that East follow suit to the red winners, so two more Diamonds are cashed and followed by two more Hearts. East follows suit to all. So South has played one Spade, four trumps, three Diamonds and three Hearts, eleven tricks in all and the lead is in dummy at Trick 12. A Spade comes and East is duly caught.

## Be very careful

| ♠ A Q 10 9 8 2 | | ♠ J 7 |
|---|---|---|
| ♡ 3 | N | ♡ A 6 5 4 2 |
| ◇ K J 10 | W   E | ◇ A Q 3 |
| ♣ A K Q | S | ♣ 10 8 6 |

Here is the same contract—more or less—, i.e.: 7♠ and the lead is a Heart. You take with the ace and follow with a trump finesse. The knave wins and North follows. What card did you play on that trick? The ♠ 8 I hope. The ♠ 7 follows and you finesse. And—I hope—play the ♠ 2 on that one. Because dummy has only two entries and if by chance South happens to hold four Spades to the king, although with the lead in your own hand at Trick 3 you can enter to shorten your trumps twice, there is no further entry, so no way to coup the outstanding trumps. The lead, with dummy so short of entries, must remain in dummy *just in case* South holds four trumps.

## Precaution

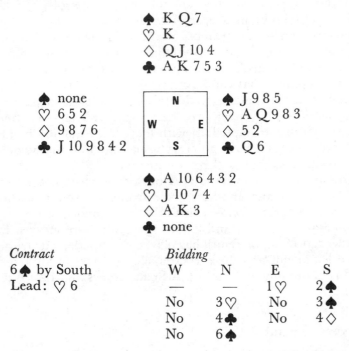

|  | ♠ K Q 7 |  |
|---|---|---|
|  | ♡ K |  |
|  | ◇ Q J 10 4 |  |
|  | ♣ A K 7 5 3 |  |

| ♠ none | | ♠ J 9 8 5 |
| ♡ 6 5 2 | | ♡ A Q 9 8 3 |
| ◇ 9 8 7 6 | | ◇ 5 2 |
| ♣ J 10 9 8 4 2 | | ♣ Q 6 |

|  | ♠ A 10 6 4 3 2 |
|  | ♡ J 10 7 4 |
|  | ◇ A K 3 |
|  | ♣ none |

| *Contract* | *Bidding* | | | |
|---|---|---|---|---|
| 6♠ by South | W | N | E | S |
| Lead: ♡ 6 | — | — | 1♡ | 2♠ |
|  | No | 3♡ | No | 3♠ |
|  | No | 4♣ | No | 4◇ |
|  | No | 6♠ | | |

North-South did quite well to reach the slam after the opening psychic and the contract appeared to be simple enough until East, winning Trick 1 with his ♡ A, followed with the ♡ Q, forcing dummy to ruff. The play immediately suggested to South the possibility of East holding four trumps, so his first action was to take advantage of being in dummy to shorten his own trumps by ruffing a low club. Back to dummy with a trump and the position was confirmed so the other Spade was played and another small Club ruffed. South now entered dummy with a small Diamond to the queen, to produce:

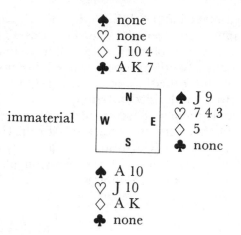

          ♠ none
          ♡ none
          ◇ J 10 4
          ♣ A K 7

immaterial

                        ♠ J 9
                        ♡ 7 4 3
                        ◇ 5
                        ♣ nonc

          ♠ A 10
          ♡ J 10
          ◇ A K
          ♣ none

Dummy now played the top Clubs, East refusing to ruff, not to
have his trumps couped, but South now discarded the ◇ A and
K and played Diamonds from dummy against which East had
no defence.

## Quadruple grand coup against left-hand opponent

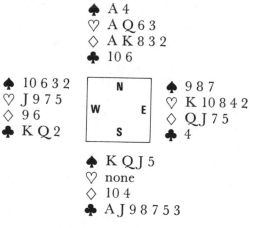

                    ♠ A 4
                    ♡ A Q 6 3
                    ◇ A K 8 3 2
                    ♣ 10 6

♠ 10 6 3 2                        ♠ 9 8 7
♡ J 9 7 5                         ♡ K 10 8 4 2
◇ 9 6                             ◇ Q J 7 5
♣ K Q 2                           ♣ 4

                    ♠ K Q J 5
                    ♡ none
                    ◇ 10 4
                    ♣ A J 9 8 7 5 3

*Contract*
6♣ by South
Doubled by West
Lead: ♡ 5

The ♡ Q was played at Trick 1, not in an endeavour to take a trick but simply to discover where the king was. Finding it with East made the vision of both trump honours with West a practical certainty. South trumped, entered dummy twice more with Diamonds and ruffed two more Hearts. On the evidence of the lead South now decided to trump his ♡ A instead of a Diamond. This left him with just three trumps and three Spades, the ♠ A having been the entry for the last ruff. He cashed the Spades, ruffing the last with dummy's ♣ 10. Now a trump, finessing the nine—at Trick 11—put West on play, forced to lead away from his other trump honour. A foolish double, heavily penalised, a double which would be fragile even at Pairs.

## Against the coup

```
                    ♠ Q 4 3
                    ♡ A J 7 6 4
                    ◇ A J 9
                    ♣ 9 4

  ♠ K 10 8 6 5         N          ♠ A J 7
  ♡ 9 8 2                         ♡ K Q 10
  ◇ 8 7 5 4       W       E       ◇ 10 3 2
  ♣ 5                             ♣ A Q 6 3
                       S
                    ♠ 9 2
                    ♡ 5 3
                    ◇ K Q 6
                    ♣ K J 10 8 7 2
```

| *Contract* | *Bidding* | | | |
|---|---|---|---|---|
| 3 ♣ by South | W | N | E | S |
| Lead: ♠ 6 | — | 1 ♡ | Dbl. | Redbl. |
| | 1 ♠ | No | No | 2 ♣ |
| | 2 ♠ | No | No | 3 ♣ |

Dummy played small at Trick 1 and East won with the knave, switching to the ♡ K, ducked by dummy. East now led a small Spade, West returning a Heart. Dummy won and South played trumps, running the ♣ 9 and following with another on which

East played the ace. The natural temptation was now to play another Spade but South was marked with no more, the defence had already won four tricks and the vital facet of the hand was to make a fifth by protecting East's ♣ Q. He therefore attacked entries by playing a Diamond.

South ruffed a Heart, shortening his holding once, entered with the Diamond ace to play a high Heart but East simply discarded a Diamond and with no further entry in dummy South had to go one down. Had East played a Spade instead of a Diamond South's trumps would have been once shortened and so one entry fewer would have been required in dummy.

The only defence against the grand coup is an attack on entries combined with the refusal to aid declarer by playing cards which enable him to shorten his trump holding.

## Deductions from the evidence: Sherlock Holmes section

*Declarer*

|   |   |   |
|---|---|---|
|   | N |   |
| W |   | E |
|   | S |   |

♠ A 7
♡ K 6 5 4 2
◇ 9 7 6
♣ 4 3 2

♠ K 9 6 5
♡ 9 8 7
◇ 8 6 4 2
♣ A 6

*Contract*
2 ◇ by West
Lead: ♣ 5

*Bidding*

| W | E |
|---|---|
| 1 ◇ | 1 ♡ |
| 1 ♠ | 2 ◇ |
| No |   |

With no score and a hand of no great significance South amuses himself with some analysis. The lead is obviously North's lowest, so he has four Clubs to a picture or so. That gives West four Clubs too, so he must be 4–1–4–4 unless void of Hearts. He made no effort so must have less than 18 points; if 16 that gives North 10. With that and five Hearts to four honours he would bid over 1 ◇, so West is not void and his singleton is likely to be the queen as even with four Hearts and 10 or more points, Hearts A Q J 10 say, North might bid. So North is 3–4–2–4. So I win my Club ace and return a trump. I shall duck when the second Spade comes from the table as West might have Q 10 and go wrong. If so we shall beat the hand. First of course West will win a trump trick and lead his ♡ Q. North will take and follow my defence with another trump. West at best can make four Diamonds, one Heart, one Spade, one ruff and perhaps another Spade or Club.

|  |  | N |  |  |
|---|---|---|---|---|
| ♠ 7 4 2 |  |  |  | ♠ A 9 6 |
| ♡ Q 9 5 | W |  | E | ♡ K 10 |
| ◇ K 7 2 |  |  |  | ◇ J 9 8 4 |
| ♣ A K Q 6 |  | S |  | ♣ J 8 7 3 |

*Contract*     *Bidding*
3 ♣ by West

| W | N | E | S |
|---|---|---|---|
| 1 ♣ | 1 ♡ | 1 NT | 2 ♡ |
| No | No | 3 ♣ |  |

Lead: ♡ A

North switches to a small Spade won by South with the queen and the suit returned to North's knave and dummy's ace. West plays the ♡ K, draws three rounds of trumps, North discarding on the third, throws dummy's losing Spade on his ♡ Q and ruffs his own Spade in dummy, North dropping the king. A Diamond now comes from dummy and West plays the king with the utmost confidence to make his contract.

South showed three small Hearts, queen to four Spades, three small Clubs. Only the possession of the ◇ A could possibly justify his bid.

*Bidding* W–E 40 on score.

| W | E |
|---|---|
| 1 ♡ | 1 ♠ |
| 2 ♡ | 3 ♣ |
| 3 NT | No |

An exercise in mental construction. West cannot hold three Spades or he would have given preference. He is unlikely to hold three Clubs or he would have passed at 40 up. He won't have four Diamonds because he failed to bid them over 1 ♠. He is probably 2–6–3–2. East sounds pretty good, pushing the auction up fearlessly. Neither of his suits however seems solid enough to play at the four-level opposite doubletons so he almost certainly has good support in Diamonds. He sounds like 5–0–3–5. How about:

| ♠ 9 2 |  | N |  | ♠ K Q 10 5 2 |
|---|---|---|---|---|
| ♡ K J 10 6 4 2 | W |  | E | ♡ none |
| ◇ A K 10 |  |  |  | ◇ Q J 6 |
| ♣ K Q |  | S |  | ♣ A J 10 6 4 |

West's conversion to 3 NT in face of at least a semi-misfit must come from a pretty good hand.

$\diamondsuit$ K 7 3

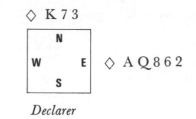

$\diamondsuit$ A Q 8 6 2

*Contract*                    *Declarer*
4 ♠ by South
Lead: $\diamondsuit$ 5

East wins with the queen as dummy plays small. The lead is either top of nothing, 5 4, a singleton or from three to a picture. South drops the $\diamondsuit$ 9. So the lead is top of nothing, either a singleton or doubleton. East can therefore confidently play the ace and give his partner a third-round ruff. The missing cards are J, 10, 4. West from J 10 5 would lead the knave. South would have done better to drop the ten rather than the nine, leaving the possibility in East's mind that the lead could have been from J 9 5. East would probably still have read it correctly however because South's card must be false; if West had J 9 5 South would normally play the 4.

| *West* | *Bidding* | | | |
|---|---|---|---|---|
| ♠ J 6 4 3 | W | N | E | S |
| ♡ 9 5 2 | — | 1 ♡ | No | 2 NT |
| $\diamondsuit$ Q 10 4 | No | 3 NT | | |
| ♣ 9 8 7 | | | | |

West must lead. But what? Firstly, if the hand is to be defeated, declarer should have reasonably minimum values. If he is loaded with points nothing will do it so the defence must assume that there is nothing serious to spare. West therefore places declarer with some 26 points. So East has 11 or so, yet passed 1 ♡. With a decent suit of Spades he might have come in at the one-level but although neither opponent is likely to have four cards in Spades, neither is he. The most likely and most hopeful possibility is that he has a five-card minor suit which, pretty weak, he was chary of bidding at the two-level. If it is Clubs it is, by that very token, bound to be stopped at least twice. But something like knave to five Diamonds might be the perfect suit to be filled by West's Q 10 and if entries are needed the right hand will have them. So it must be a Diamond lead. Which? Probably anything could be right at any time but perhaps an unusual card might help. To lead the queen might well deceive declarer into placing the length in the wrong hand and take a two-way finesse to East. Nothing sure about this but a play based on fair logic is bound to succeed quite frequently.

| West | Bidding | | | |
|------|---------|---|---|---|
| ♠ A 8 4 | W | N | E | S |
| ♡ A J 10 9 7 | No | 1♣ | No | 1♢ |
| ♢ 5 4 | 1♡ | 1♠ | No | 2♢ |
| ♣ J 6 3 | No | 3♢ | No | 3 NT |

West must lead. The standard lead from such a suit is the ♡ J, top of the interior sequence. West considers the bidding. South must have a fair hand, not good because of the simple rebid of 2♢ but apparently good enough to accept an invitation. He did not bid 1 NT so is unlikely to hold both missing honours in Hearts; he probably downgraded a ♡ K after hearing West's bid. To lead the ♡ J in such circumstances might therefore be disastrous; all right if partner has the queen but no good if North has it. Yet North bid two suits and supported a third. If North has it the likelihood is that it will be singleton. West leads the ♡ A.

|  | | |
|---|---|---|
| ♠ A 10 8 4 2 | **N** | ♠ K Q 5 3 |
| ♡ K 3 2 | | ♡ A |
| ♢ A 10 8 4 | **W    E** | ♢ 6 5 4 3 |
| ♣ K | **S** | ♣ A J 4 3 |

| Contract | Bidding | | | |
|----------|---------|---|---|---|
| 6♠ by West | W | N | E | S |
| Lead: ♡ 9 | — | — | 1♣ | 3♡ |
| | 3♠ | No | 4♠ | 5♢ |
| | Dbl. | 5♡ | No | No |
| | 6♠ | | | |

East's pass of 5♡ must be a forcing pass here, indicating that he is prepared for a contract of 5♠ if West prefers that to a double of 5♡. West, with strength to spare, decided that the small slam should be a good proposition, encouraged by North's preference to Hearts and now assured that the opponents cannot take the first two tricks with the ♡ A and a ruff. Dummy's four small Diamonds provide a slight shock but reference to the bidding reassures him. North must be void, for South could hardly bid as he did with fewer than eleven red cards. Dummy's ace wins Trick 1 and trumps are drawn in three rounds, South having the singleton. The ♣ K is unblocked (vital), the ◊ A cashed to verify North's void, and then comes the ♡ K and a Heart ruff. The hands are now:

| ♠ 10 8 | N | ♠ none |
|---|---|---|
| ♡ none | W E | ♡ none |
| ◊ 10 8 4 | | ◊ 6 5 |
| ♣ none | S | ♣ A J 4 |

Dummy, on play, simply leads the small Club, taken by North, the only other player holding Clubs and, as he has nothing else, he must play another, enabling West to take the marked finesse, thus getting rid of his three small Diamonds on dummy's last three Clubs.

## Exception to the rule

♠ K Q 7 6
♡ 8 4
◊ A 9 7
♣ A 8 6 2

| N | ♠ J 10 8 4 |
|---|---|
| W E | ♡ K Q 5 |
| | ◊ 5 |
| S | ♣ K Q J 9 5 |

*Contract*
7 ◊ by South
Lead: ♠ 3

*Bidding*

| | S | N | |
|---|---|---|---|
| | 2 ◊ | 2 ♠ | |
| | 3 ◊ | 4 ◊ | |
| (conv) | 4 NT | 5 ♡ | two aces |
| | 6 ◊ | 7 ◊ | |

North has a good hand but seems to have taken a bit of a liberty with that last bid. East wonders if the hand might be beaten. The lead is an obvious doubleton. West is not leading low from a picture because he hasn't got one, and he must have one more card because if he hadn't South would have four and they would by playing in Spades rather than Diamonds.

South wins Trick 1 in hand and plays four rounds of trumps, West discarding his ♠ 2, dummy a Heart on the fourth round. East throws a Club and a Heart but then must huddle. He builds up South's hand. Ace to three Spades, six Diamonds, a single Club—must be; he couldn't bid 4 NT for aces with a small doubleton; he would perforce cue-bid Hearts instead. So he must have ace to three Hearts. So he has only eleven top tricks. (6 ◇ was obviously the right spot—give up a Heart and ruff one; simple—.) East realises that he is being subjected to a squeeze over three suits. If South has the ♡ J and East throws a Club, the play will go ♣ A, Club ruff, ♠ K and Club ruff, ♠ Q, the lead in dummy and the position:

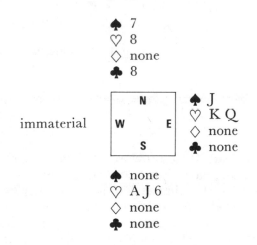

```
                        ♠ 7
                        ♡ 8
                        ◇ none
                        ♣ 8

                      N              ♠ J
                                     ♡ K Q
   immaterial      W      E          ◇ none
                                     ♣ none
                      S

                        ♠ none
                        ♡ A J 6
                        ◇ none
                        ♣ none
```

The play of dummy's established long Club will, while enabling South to throw his small Heart, force East to throw his winning Spade or blank his ♡ K. There is no defence therefore if he throws a Club, while, if he throws a Spade, the position will be identical except that a winning Spade will come at Trick 11 instead of a winning Club. So a black suit discard is useless.

East doesn't bother to analyse the situation further but simply discards a Heart picture.

This would of course also fail if South had the ♡ 10 as well as the knave but he did not have it, West hung on manfully to his Heart guard and at Trick 13 made his ten.

Process of elimination is useful indeed; if everything else is useless simply try what is left. It may also be useless but sometimes it isn't. In the upshot South blamed North for bidding seven. North pointed out that South didn't have his 2 ◇ bid. Did he?

### Killing the entries

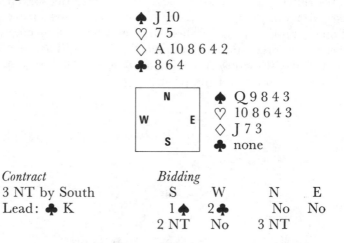

```
          ♠ J 10
          ♡ 7 5
          ◇ A 10 8 6 4 2
          ♣ 8 6 4

              N          ♠ Q 9 8 4 3
        W         E      ♡ 10 8 6 4 3
              S          ◇ J 7 3
                         ♣ none
```

| Contract | Bidding | | | |
|---|---|---|---|---|
| 3 NT by South | S | W | N | E |
| Lead: ♣ K | 1♠ | 2♣ | No | No |
| | 2 NT | No | 3 NT | |

South ducks the lead. West switches to the ♠ 2 which to East appears to be a singleton. So what is West doing? East thinks about it and realises that that ♠ J 10 is a sure entry to dummy by a concession of the ♠ Q. West is killing the entry for the Diamonds. East obediently ducks. South comes to hand with the ♡ A and plays the ◇ 9. West plays small, dummy the ◇ 10. East ducks that as well. With only two Diamonds unaccounted for, the others must have one each and the entire suit will be good if he takes that trick.

# The full hands

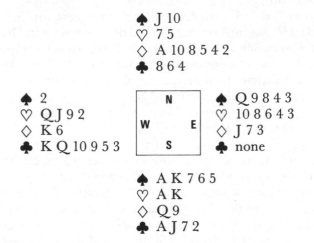

```
                        ♠ J 10
                        ♡ 7 5
                        ◇ A 10 8 5 4 2
                        ♣ 8 6 4
♠ 2                                        ♠ Q 9 8 4 3
♡ Q J 9 2              N                   ♡ 10 8 6 4 3
◇ K 6            W           E             ◇ J 7 3
♣ K Q 10 9 5 3          S                  ♣ none
                        ♠ A K 7 6 5
                        ♡ A K
                        ◇ Q 9
                        ♣ A J 7 2
```

West's switch to Spades was brilliant. Both ducks by East were good solid work. West's play of a small Diamond was not so hot. The king was the right shot, taking the pressure off his partner. South's ◇ 9 was brilliant, the only possible play with a chance to win. But South killed himself at Trick 1. The duck was instinctive reaction; a lack of consideration at Trick 1. Please check that nine tricks are made if South wins Trick 1.

# Co-operation at Pairs—and its lack

```
♠ A 6 4              N              ♠ K Q 8
♡ A Q 10                            ♡ 7 5 2
◇ Q J 10 9      W           E       ◇ A 8 6 4
♣ A Q 2              S              ♣ K J 10
```

| *Contract* | *Bidding* | |
|---|---|---|
| 6 NT by West | W | E |
| Lead: ♠ J | 1 ◇ | 1 ♡ |
| | 3 NT | 6 NT |

An odd bid from East, not crazy—just odd—but over 3 NT to go straight to 6 NT is stretching it a bit; with a five-card suit—all right—but balanced hands opposite balanced have gaps and are subject to duplication, as with the Clubs here where five top honours produce only three tricks.

West took Trick 1 with his ace and unsuccessfully finessed Diamonds. He was now reduced to the double finesse in Hearts. Taking the next Spade he finessed the ♡ 10, winning. He now played off his winners, ending in dummy at Trick 11 to take the second Heart finesse. Dummy played the ♡ 5, South the ♡ 9, West took out the Heart queen and then put it back to play the ace, duly dropping North's king and making his contract. Check that this was the correct play.

North, playing match-pointed Pairs had decided to play for two down to ensure a top on the board, so had reduced his holding to the ♡ K alone and the thirteenth Club. The real clue, however, was a small Heart from South. If the double finesse actually was on, that card should have been the knave, and South, who should have known precisely what was going on—because if West had the ♡ K he would have claimed his contract at Trick 5—was entirely to blame for the disaster.

| *Declarer* | | *Dummy* |
|---|---|---|
| | | ♠ K 9 7 6 3 2 |
| | N | ♡ A J 4 3 |
| W | | E |
| | S | ♢ 9 4 |
| | | ♣ 7 |

♠ A J 8
♡ 10 8 5
♢ A K Q 2
♣ A 6 4

| *Contract* | *Bidding* | | | |
|---|---|---|---|---|
| 2♡ by West | S | W | N | E |
| Lead: ♢ 8 | 1♢ | No | No | 1♠ |
| | 1 NT | No | 2♣ | No |
| | No | 2♡ | | |

North leads the ♢ 8. The content of the West and North hands is not our serious concern and the result is unimportant. We just want to see what South can learn from dummy and from the lead.

The ♢ 8 is the top of nothing. Higher cards missing are J and

10 and with those the lead would be the J; with one of them a small card from length or the honour from a doubleton. North almost certainly has three cards in Diamonds. He can't have four or he would simply have converted 1 NT to 2 ◇, not 2 ♣. What about West? He passed 1 NT yet came in over 2 ♣. The only reason for this is the increase of information. That in turn can only be through the possession of length in Clubs. North should have five, South three when he bids 1 NT, so it looks as if West expected that singleton in his dummy. So he himself has four Clubs, and certainly four Diamonds. Then he bids 2 ♡; only the knowledge that shortage in Clubs faced him and therefore the likelihood of some length in Hearts, enabled him to make the bid on his four-card suit. He is therefore 1–4–4–4, single Spade. For honours he probably has some 10 points if we allow 4 to North: more probably 11, three kings and a queen should be about right.

## A laydown

♠ Q 4
♡ A K 8 6 5
◇ A K Q 4 2
♣ A

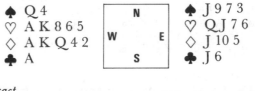

♠ J 9 7 3
♡ Q J 7 6
◇ J 10 5
♣ J 6

*Contract*
6 ♡ by West
Lead: ♣ 5

West–East reach a somewhat dubious small slam after North opens the bidding with a pre-emptive 3 ♠. On the lead the contract must be ice cold. Please check this.

West wins the opening lead with his single ace and draws trumps in two rounds. He enters dummy with the ◇ J and ruffs dummy's small Club. He now plays a few Diamonds—enough— and then leads a small Spade away from his queen.

North could hardly hold both tops in Spades or he would have led one of them. He must have at least six cards in the suit so South has a singleton, either the ace or the king. If he takes this trick he must concede a ruff-and-discard and if North takes it he will crash the honours together, establishing West's queen.

**Bread-and-jam**

1    ♠ A 10 8 7 6 2              ♠ K Q J 6
       ♡ 7 4                   ♡ A K 5

       ◇ A 9                  ◇ Q 3

       ♣ K 5 2                 ♣ A Q 6 4

*Hand 1.* South opens 3 ◇. West plays 7 ♠. *Lead:* ◇ 6.

2    ♠ none                ♠ 8 3
      ♡ A Q 8 6 4 2         ♡ K J 10 9

      ◇ K Q 4 2            ◇ A 9 8 5

      ♣ A 6 2               ♣ K 8 3

*Hand 2.* West plays 6 ♡. *Lead:* ♠ A.

*Hand 1.* South's Diamonds are hardly solid so he surely has seven of them. West takes Trick 1 with his ace and views his chances. The contract is safe if Clubs break evenly but this is unlikely in view of South's shape. When South follows to two trumps and one Heart North is marked with ten cards in Clubs and Hearts, South with at most four. So it is likely that a squeeze can operate, using Hearts as the controlling suit, the ◇ 9 and dummy's fourth Clubs as the one-card menaces. West tests the Clubs, finding five with North which means that both defenders guard Hearts. He comes down to three cards:

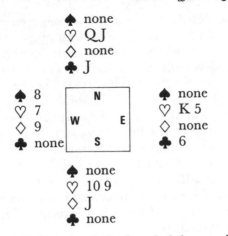

```
           ♠ none
           ♡ Q J
           ◇ none
           ♣ J

  ♠ 8      ┌─────────┐    ♠ none
  ♡ 7      │    N    │    ♡ K 5
  ◇ 9      │ W     E │    ◇ none
  ♣ none   │    S    │    ♣ 6
           └─────────┘
           ♠ none
           ♡ 10 9
           ◇ J
           ♣ none
```

The last trump leaves the defenders helpless, neither able to retain a guard in Hearts while keeping their outside master cards.

*Hand 2.* Trumps are drawn, ruffing out dummy's second Spade on the way and a safety-play in Diamonds is made. The ◇ K is cashed and a defender put on play with the third Club. With no further Diamond he must concede a ruff-and-discard; if he started with four, he must lead one, either permitting the ◇ 8 to win or setting up a finesse position against his second honour. Check the importance of cashing one Diamond.

```
3  ♠ K Q 2      ┌─────────┐    ♠ A 9 3
   ♡ A Q J 10 4 │    N    │    ♡ 7 5 3 2
   ◇ 8 5 3      │ W     E │    ◇ J 7 2
   ♣ K 5        │    S    │    ♣ A J 7
                └─────────┘
```

*Hand 3.* West plays 4♡. The defence cash three Diamonds and switch to a Spade.

```
4  ♠ A Q 3      ┌─────────┐    ♠ 5 4
   ♡ 9 7 5      │    N    │    ♡ A K Q
   ◇ A 8 7 5 3  │ W     E │    ◇ K 4 2
   ♣ Q J        │    S    │    ♣ A K 10 8 3
                └─────────┘
```

*Hand 4.* West plays 6 NT. *Lead:* ♡ J.

*Hand 3.* The ♠ 9 should be played just in case it holds. It doesn't so West goes to dummy with the ♠ A and takes the trump finesse. North shows void. Two more entries are needed in order to pick up South's king so West plays a small Club and finesses the knave, which wins, takes the trump finesse again, overtakes his ♣ K with the ace and takes the third trump finesse.

*And 3A.* Could the defence have done better?

*Hand 4.* The choice West has is whether to try for his twelfth trick through Diamond length or a Spade finesse. Clearly he must try the Diamonds first because if that fails the Spade finesse may still be taken. But standard procedure of simply ducking a round of Diamonds is very dangerous. Should South win the trick he will play a Spade and now West is faced with the choice of finessing at once, still not knowing whether Diamond break or not. The answer is simple. The *second* round of Diamonds is ducked.

*And 3A.* Yes, the defence was asleep. North, appreciating that his partner sat with a guard in trumps should have played the ♣ Q on the first round of the suit, reducing dummy's entries by one and thus defeating the contract.

5
| | ♠ 10 7 6 5 3 2 | | | ♠ Q 4 |
| | ♡ A 6 3 | N | | ♡ K Q |
| | ◇ Q J 10 | W   E | | ◇ A 7 5 |
| | ♣ 8 | S | | ♣ K 9 7 6 4 3 |

*Hand 5.* North opens the bidding with 1♡ but West plays the hand in 4♠. *Lead:* ♡ 4.

6
| | ♠ 2 | | | ♠ A 9 6 3 |
| | ♡ A Q 3 | N | | ♡ K 4 |
| | ◇ 10 4 2 | W   E | | ◇ A K J 5 |
| | ♣ A Q 9 7 5 2 | S | | ♣ 10 8 6 |

*Hand 6.* West plays in 6♣. *Lead:* ♠ K.

*Hand 5.* The Diamond finesse should succeed against the opening bidder. The danger therefore is that we may lose three tricks in trumps. The only positions which will enable us to keep the loss to two tricks are: ♠ A K 4, A J, K J with North.

The common factor is that the knave must be doubleton. So although in a World Final the player played a trump from dummy at Trick 2, we must not. The play at Trick 2 is a Club—

any Club, preparing to ruff one as an entry to play trumps from the West hand.

*Hand 6.* There are two basic ways to handle this trump suit: the finesse of the queen, hoping to lose no trick, or the safety-play of the ace first and then a small card led towards the queen. The decision however must be delayed for there is also a Diamond finesse situation which cannot be avoided. So the Diamond finesse is taken first. If it fails the trump suit must be played for no loser; if it wins we may take the safety-play in trumps.

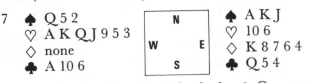

7    ♠ Q 5 2        ♠ A K J
       ♡ A K Q J 9 5 3       ♡ 10 6
       ◇ none           ◇ K 8 7 6 4
       ♣ A 10 6        ♣ Q 5 4

*Hand 7.* West plays 6♡. North leads the ◇ Q not covered but ruffed by West. He plays the ♡ A and then small to dummy's ♡ 10 to ruff a second Diamond. North drops the ◇ J. West draws the last trump, getting a bit short, South having started with four but West now enters dummy with a Spade to ruff another Diamond, North discarding this time. West plays a second Spade, all following. The contract is now safe. Because?

8    ♠ J 8 3        ♠ 7
       ♡ A Q J 8       ♡ K 2
       ◇ A 5           ◇ Q 7 3 2
       ♣ K J 10 3       ♣ A Q 9 7 6 2

*Hand 8.* South opens the bidding with 1♠ but West still reaches a contract of 6♣. North leads the ♠ 9 taken by South with the queen. He switches to a Heart.

*Hand 7.* South has shown six cards in Diamonds, four in Hearts and followed to two Spades. He therefore cannot hold more than a single Club and could even be void. West therefore cashes the ♣ A to cater for a single king and plays small toward the queen. Dummy still has a master Spade so North must concede the rest.

*Hand 8.* West takes the Heart in dummy and draws trumps, using the high cards in his own hand. He now ruffs a small Spade (although this is technically unnecessary as it may just as well be discarded on a long trump) cashes four Hearts and plays off his remaining trumps. The final position is:

immaterial

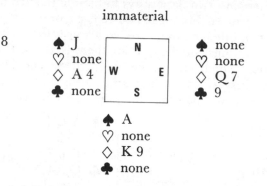

8  ♠ J         ♠ none
   ♡ none      ♡ none
   ◇ A 4       ◇ Q 7
   ♣ none      ♣ 9

   ♠ A
   ♡ none
   ◇ K 9
   ♣ none

and South is helpless when the last trump comes.

9  ♠ A 8            ♠ J 6 3 2
   ♡ A Q 5 2        ♡ 7 4
   ◇ A K Q 10       ◇ 8 7 3
   ♣ K 9 5          ♣ A 6 4 2

*Hand 9.* West, opening a conventional 2 ♣, gets to 3 NT. *Lead:* ♡ 3.

10  ♠ 4 2           ♠ K 7
    ♡ A Q 10 8 4    ♡ K J 9 7 3
    ◇ 6 4 2         ◇ A Q 10 8
    ♣ A K 7         ♣ 6 2

*Hand 10.* West plays in 4 ♡. *Lead:* ♠ Q.

*Hand 9.* West seeks his ninth trick. He takes the jack with the ♡ Q and ducks a round of Clubs. He ducks the second Heart but takes the third and plays the ♠ 8 to South's 9. South plays a Diamond. West takes it and plays his last Heart to North who exits with the ♠ 10. West cashes Clubs but South shows out on the third round so West finesses the ◇ 10 for his ninth trick. He made one mistake.

*Hand 10.* The danger here is the loss of two Spades and two Diamonds. West tries to leave South on play at Trick 2. He can then draw trumps, eliminate Clubs, and end-play South by taking a Diamond finesse. So he ducks the ♠ Q. North switches to a Diamond. So?

*Hand 9.* Yes, West made one small mistake. His count of the hand strongly indicated that South held four Diamonds but he should have cashed a second one before testing Clubs. He would then have been quite sure that North did not hold the jack.

*Hand 10.* The end-play is still there. The ◇ A is played, trumps drawn, Clubs eliminated and then the ♠ K puts South on play, anything but a Diamond up to dummy's queen enforcing a ruff-and-discard.

| 11 | ♠ A Q J 10 7 3 |   | ♠ K 6 |
|----|----------------|---|-------|
|    | ♡ 3 |   | ♡ A 10 9 7 4 |
|    | ◇ 10 8 2 | W    E | ◇ A K 5 |
|    | ♣ A 10 6 |   | ♣ K Q 4 |

*Hand 11.* North leads the ♡ K against ♠ 6 by West.

| 12 | ♠ A Q 5 |   | ♠ 8 7 4 2 |
|----|---------|---|-----------|
|    | ♡ A J 10 7 5 2 |   | ♡ K Q 6 |
|    | ◇ 6 2 | W    E | ◇ K Q 7 4 |
|    | ♣ K 3 |   | ♣ 5 4 |

*Hand 12.* South opens 1♣ and over West's 1 ♡ North bids 1♠. West reaches 4♡. North leads a Club taken by South's ace and the ♠ 3 is returned.

*Hand 11.* Both the minor suits are duplicated in length so there is no chance for any manipulation. There are twelve tricks and no more. West should therefore ensure that they do not turn into eleven. He ducks the opening lead. The losing Diamond can be discarded on the ♡ A after trumps have been drawn.

*Hand 12.* This Spade from South is an obvious singleton. There are no tenaces into which South can be forced to play. The only solution is that South must be made to give a ruff-and-discard on something. That something can only be Diamonds. Trumps will have to be split two-two. West plays a Diamond to the King which wins. South is holding up so West does not bother to waste entries for this hand is going down at speed if North has that ace; West plays the ◇ Q. South takes and exits with a Club. Dummy is entered with a trump and a Diamond is ruffed. Dummy is entered with another trump and the fourth Diamond played, South producing the knave on which West discards one of his losing Spades. South with nothing left but Clubs has to play one. West discards his last Spade and ruffs in dummy.

# Squeeze Play

**Simple positional**

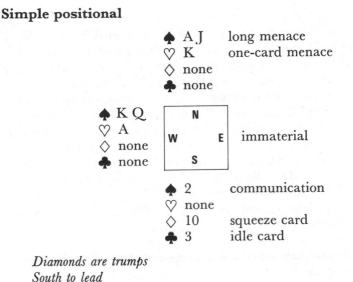

| | | |
|---|---|---|
| ♠ | A J | long menace |
| ♡ | K | one-card menace |
| ◇ | none | |
| ♣ | none | |

♠ K Q
♡ A
◇ none
♣ none     immaterial

| | | |
|---|---|---|
| ♠ | 2 | communication |
| ♡ | none | |
| ◇ | 10 | squeeze card |
| ♣ | 3 | idle card |

*Diamonds are trumps*
*South to lead*

South leads the ◇ 10 and West must either discard his ace or unguard Spades. The squeeze operates because West has no idle card which he can throw. A basic principle of squeeze play is therefore that all idle cards should be removed from the opponents' hands before the squeeze card is played.

## Requirements for the simple positional squeeze

A two-card menace and a one-card menace sitting over the player to be squeezed. (The long menaces may be extended but a one-card and a two-card menace provide the absolute minimum for the coup to be operative.)

A squeeze card in the hand opposite to the menaces, i.e.: a card to which the victim cannot follow suit.

A card of communication to the long menace opposite.

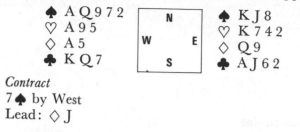

♠ A Q 9 7 2
♡ A 9 5
◇ A 5
♣ K Q 7

♠ K J 8
♡ K 7 4 2
◇ Q 9
♣ A J 6 2

*Contract*
7♠ by West
Lead: ◇ J

There are twelve tricks on top and apparently no play for a thirteenth. Dummy's Clubs provide one discard but West needs two unless North is leading away from the ◇ K, most unlikely against a grand slam. There is however the chance for a squeeze. When the ◇ A has gone we have a one-card menace against somebody and if that same player has four cards in Hearts we may be able to squeeze him. We can play off one Diamond, four Clubs and five Spades—ten tricks, coming down to one Diamond and two Hearts in the West hand and three Hearts in the East hand. Obviously at that stage, an opponent with the master Diamond and four cards in Hearts has already discarded one Heart to remain in control of both suits but now has to find another discard, which will be fatal. The only choice we have to make is whether to squeeze North or South.

The key to these situations is to picture the ending. If we play to squeeze North, the end position, assuming Trick 1 goes J, Q, K, A, will be:

♠ none
♡ Q J 10
◇ 10
♣ none

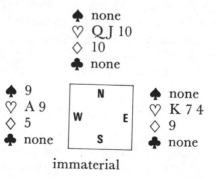

♠ 9
♡ A 9
◇ 5
♣ none

♠ none
♡ K 7 4
◇ 9
♣ none

immaterial

On the lead of the squeeze card, the ♠ 9, North must discard and dummy simply throws from the other suit. If we decide to squeeze South, the ◇ Q will not be played at Trick 1 and the end position will be:

immaterial

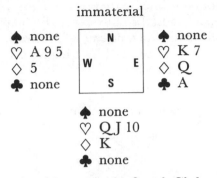

Now the squeeze card becomes the fourth Club and South must either throw his master Diamond or unguard Hearts.

We may note that there is a technical difference in this situation. The requirements for the simple positional squeeze are not fully complied with. The one-card menace, the ◇ Q, no longer sits over the victim. There is no trouble for the declarer here because in the previous simple positional situation he held an idle card, so it can be replaced by a busy card without affecting the coup. What we have actually done here is to transform our simple positional squeeze into a simple automatic.

**Simple automatic squeeze**

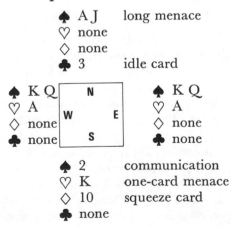

The one-card menace is now in the same hand as the squeeze card, the idle card shifted across, still idle. The position is now automatic in that it does not matter which of the defenders holds the vital cards; he must be squeezed. This happens because North has an idle card which he can safely throw. (That ♣ 3 is not a winner but a loser, covered by a higher Club in the hand which is not being squeezed.)

**Simple automatic plus Vienna Coup**

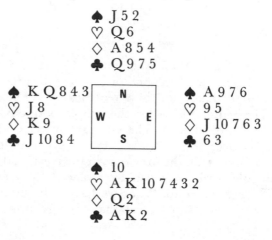

```
              ♠ J 5 2
              ♡ Q 6
              ◇ A 8 5 4
              ♣ Q 9 7 5

♠ K Q 8 4 3    ┌─────────┐    ♠ A 9 7 6
♡ J 8          │    N    │    ♡ 9 5
◇ K 9          │ W     E │    ◇ J 10 7 6 3
♣ J 10 8 4     │    S    │    ♣ 6 3
               └─────────┘
              ♠ 10
              ♡ A K 10 7 4 3 2
              ◇ Q 2
              ♣ A K 2
```

*Contract*
6 ♡ by South
Lead: ♠ K

South ruffs the second Spade and draws trumps. The contract is safe if Clubs break evenly but, if not, an extra chance can be created by cashing the Diamond ace—a Vienna Coup—leaving the isolated queen as a one-card menace against a player who might hold the ◇ K and also four Clubs. As this one-card menace will be in the same hand as the squeeze card—obviously enough the last trump—such a squeeze will operate against either defender. Dummy will come down to four Clubs and nothing else so a player with four Clubs cannot hold a Diamond as well. Declarer will have that Diamond menace and only three Clubs to hold. The situation can be reduced by playing off two rounds of Clubs, leaving dummy with two cards only after the last trump is played, declarer holding one Diamond and his card of communication, a small Club.

## Double positional matrix

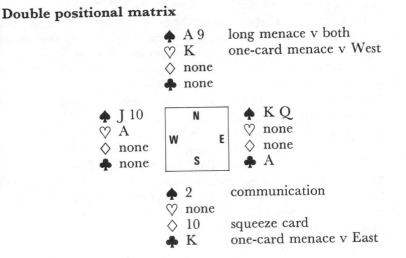

The long menace is automatic against both defenders but the one-card menace against West is positional. That against East, in the same hand as the squeeze card, is automatic but interchange the defenders' aces and the squeeze would fail. West would be squeezed out of his Spade guard but East with the ♡ A sitting over dummy's ♡ K would simply discard whatever dummy discarded.

## Rectification of the "count": technical approaches

```
     ♠ K J 8 7    ┌─────────┐    ♠ A 4 2
     ♡ K J 9 2    │    N    │    ♡ A
     ◇ A Q J      │ W     E │    ◇ K 7 5
     ♣ 8 3        │    S    │    ♣ A K J 9 7 4
                  └─────────┘
```

*Contract*
6 NT by West
Lead: ♡ 4

South plays the ♡ 5 while West examines the hand and wishes he had the ♣ Q instead of the ◇ A. The lead looks orthodox.

North might have a five-carder, South playing his lowest, or a four-carder with South using a low peter to show four. Had North led from shortage South's card would have been more encouraging.

West plays the ♣ A, intending—correctly—to finesse the knave on the second round but when South shows void must replan the hand. North is getting pretty short of Spades and Diamonds; a squeeze against him should not be difficult once the count is rectified. West plays king and ace of Diamonds. North follows, so cannot have more than two Spades. West decides to rectify the count by losing a Spade trick. He takes the standard safety-play, king first, the ace, then small towards knave. North drops the queen on the second round so his hand is now marked 2–4–2–5. This doesn't make any difference. West would have been happy to see South win with that queen later. He plays the third round of the suit and gives South his trick. Now North's idle cards have been removed and South exits with another Spade.

The position is:

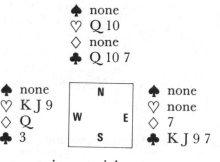

                    ♠ none
                    ♡ Q 10
                    ◇ none
                    ♣ Q 10 7

    ♠ none          ┌─────────┐          ♠ none
    ♡ K J 9         │    N    │          ♡ none
    ◇ Q             │ W     E │          ◇ 7
    ♣ 3             │    S    │          ♣ K J 9 7
                    └─────────┘

                    immaterial

South plays a Heart which West wins with his king. West now leads the ◇ Q and North is helpless. A Club discard being obviously fatal he throws his Heart queen and West suddenly finds that he needs only two tricks in Clubs instead of his initial hope for six.

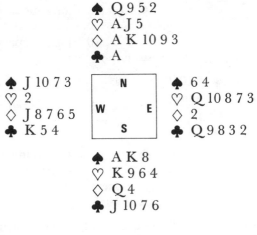

♠ Q 9 5 2
♡ A J 5
◇ A K 10 9 3
♣ A

♠ J 10 7 3          ♠ 6 4
♡ 2                 ♡ Q 10 8 7 3
◇ J 8 7 6 5         ◇ 2
♣ K 5 4             ♣ Q 9 8 3 2

♠ A K 8
♡ K 9 6 4
◇ Q 4
♣ J 10 7 6

*Pairs*
*Contract*
6 NT by South
Lead: ♡ 2

This looks like the world's worst contract but it isn't really.
People prefer no-trumps to minor suits when playing Pairs and
we need only a break and a finesse to make this. Both wrong as
it happens but then they are also both wrong if we play in 6 ◇,
6 ♡ or 6 ♠; also seven-trump contracts being worse. The lead
anyway is fortunate although that break and finesse, were we
right, produce twelve tricks against any lead.

Dummy played small and South's king took East's ten. He
played another, expecting the Heart length to be on his left and
was somewhat taken aback when it wasn't. He played the ace,
came to hand with the ◇ Q and took the ◇ 10 finesse, East
showing out. Not really open to criticism, that, as East must
have a few Clubs and has plenty of Hearts. South gave up a
Heart trick to East's queen, establishing his ♡ 9. East got off
play with a Club to dummy's ace.

This, for a reputedly first-class player was crass idiocy; the
duty of a defender is to block the declarer's suits, not to unblock
them. East could see that dummy was sitting over West with
menacing strings of Diamonds and Spades. The possibility of a
squeeze was screaming at him. He probably wasn't listening.
South came back with a Spade and completely ruined West
with the fourth round of Hearts.

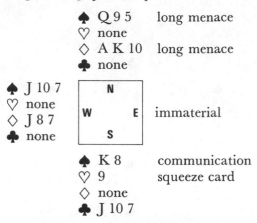

♠ Q 9 5      long menace
♡ none
◇ A K 10     long menace
♣ none

♠ J 10 7
♡ none
◇ J 8 7
♣ none

immaterial

♠ K 8        communication
♡ 9          squeeze card
◇ none
♣ J 10 7

On the lead of the ♡ 9 West is helpless and North simply discards from the suit which West retains. The position can be reduced to a three-card situation by cashing two top Diamonds and king of Spades. The ◇ 10 now gives us a simple one-card menace sitting over West, the ♠ Q 9 the minimum long menace similarly placed.

Had East played another Heart instead of that thoughtless Club West could have discarded a Club. Dummy itself would have been squeezed, forced to discard either a Spade or a Diamond. The defensive error set up a straightforward simple positional squeeze.

**Double positional**

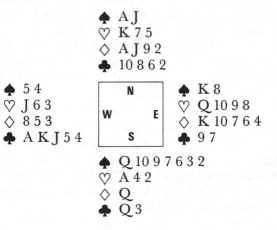

♠ A J
♡ K 7 5
◇ A J 9 2
♣ 10 8 6 2

♠ 5 4
♡ J 6 3
◇ 8 5 3
♣ A K J 5 4

♠ K 8
♡ Q 10 9 8
◇ K 10 7 6 4
♣ 9 7

♠ Q 10 9 7 6 3 2
♡ A 4 2
◇ Q
♣ Q 3

*Contract*
4♠ by South
Lead: ♣ A

East calls with the ♣ 9, the king follows and then West switches
to the ◇ 8 taken by the ace. South ruffs a Diamond and takes
the Spade finesse which is wrong and a Spade comes back. He
ruffs a Club and plays trumps to reach this position:

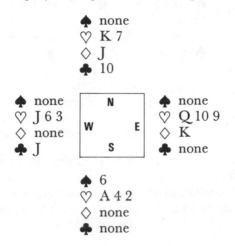

The last trump is the squeeze-card. West, menaced by the ♣ 10,
has to throw a Heart. The ♣ 10 has now done its work so is
discarded. The pressure passes to East who, menaced by the ◇ J
in dummy, also must throw a Heart, South takes the last three
tricks with Hearts. This is a simultaneous double squeeze,
squeezing both opponents at the same trick.

## Double automatic matrix—simultaneous situation

&spades; A K 10    long menace *v* both
&hearts; 8          idle card
&diams; none
&clubs; none

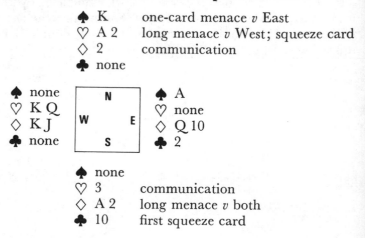

&spades; Q 3 2          &spades; J 5 4
&hearts; A               &hearts; none
&diams; none             &diams; none
&clubs; none             &clubs; A

&spades; 6        communication
&hearts; K        one-card menace *v* either
&diams; 10        squeeze card
&clubs; K        one-card menace *v* either

The two aces held by the defenders may be interchanged but
without effect. Once both one-card menaces are in the same
hand as the squeeze card there is no defence. On the play of the
&diams; 10 West must let go a Spade, dummy throwing the idle card.
Now East must either unguard Spades as well or establish
South's &clubs; K.

## Double automatic matrix—interrupted situation

&spades; K        one-card menace *v* East
&hearts; A 2      long menace *v* West; squeeze card
&diams; 2        communication
&clubs; none

&spades; none          &spades; A
&hearts; K Q            &hearts; none
&diams; K J            &diams; Q 10
&clubs; none            &clubs; 2

&spades; none
&hearts; 3        communication
&diams; A 2      long menace *v* both
&clubs; 10        first squeeze card

At least a four-card situation as two squeeze cards are required. The first is led, the ♣ 10, forcing West to throw a Diamond. East simply follows suit while dummy's ♡ 2, having done its work of forcing West to retain a guard in that suit, is also discarded. South now leads to the ♡ A and this becomes the second squeeze-card. West is out of the game; East, forced to retain his ♠ A by the menace of dummy's ♠ K in his turn must throw a Diamond and communication is there to enable South to cash his two Diamonds.

## Triple squeeze matrix

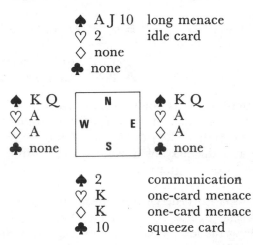

| ♠ A J 10 | long menace |
| ♡ 2 | idle card |
| ◇ none | |
| ♣ none | |

| ♠ K Q | | ♠ K Q |
| ♡ A | | ♡ A |
| ◇ A | | ◇ A |
| ♣ none | | ♣ none |

| ♠ 2 | communication |
| ♡ K | one-card menace |
| ◇ K | one-card menace |
| ♣ 10 | squeeze card |

The triple squeeze, of one opponent over three suits, brings in not one but two extra tricks. It may occur when one defender holds all the adverse strength—has opened the bidding, made an informatory double, bid strongly opposite a silent partner etc.

Here the long menace is of three cards while both one-card menaces are in the same hand as the squeeze card. The position is automatic no matter which defender holds the three guards. South plays the squeeze card and throws dummy's idle card. One ace must be thrown lest dummy be made good immediately. That ace establishes a king with South which is then played and an automatic simple squeeze results, each squeeze bringing in one extra trick.

With a two-card long menace the situation changes considerably.

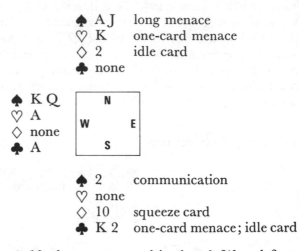

```
              ♠ A J    long menace
              ♡ K      one-card menace
              ◇ 2      idle card
              ♣ none

  ♠ K Q           N
  ♡ A
  ◇ none      W       E
  ♣ A             S

              ♠ 2      communication
              ♡ none
              ◇ 10     squeeze card
              ♣ K 2    one-card menace; idle card
```

Now when the ◇ 10, the squeeze card is played, West defeats the squeeze provided he refrains from establishing a menace held on his right. The discard of a Club would establish that menace and the play of it would simply squeeze him again. But if he throws a guard the menace against which is held on his left, the squeeze fails. He throws the ♡ A. All South can do is play a Spade. True he now makes the ♡ K but he remains with a losing Spade. Alternatively West may discard a Spade establishing the long menace on his left—providing it is of two-card, not three-card length. Again South plays a Spade and cashes a second Spade, but upon this West simply discards the ace which was menaced on his right and keeps the guard against the hand on lead.

It is a basic rule of defence against the triple squeeze to discard from a suit menaced on the left. (This assumes that the squeeze card is a master and not in process of transferring the lead to the opposite hand.)

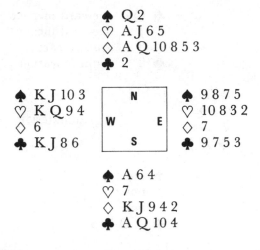

♠ Q 2
♡ A J 6 5
◇ A Q 10 8 5 3
♣ 2

♠ K J 10 3          ♠ 9 8 7 5
♡ K Q 9 4          ♡ 10 8 3 2
◇ 6                    ◇ 7
♣ K J 8 6          ♣ 9 7 5 3

♠ A 6 4
♡ 7
◇ K J 9 4 2
♣ A Q 10 4

*Contract*
7 ◇ by South
Lead: ♡ K

West opened the bidding with 1 ♣ but North-South reached the grand slam, to an extent under the impression that the opening bid was psychic. The exposure of dummy revealed that this might not be so. The lead was unfortunate to the extent that it removed the one entry which would be vital to a normal squeeze so South decided to play for a triple, ruffing two Hearts only in his own hand, giving him eight tricks in trumps and three aces, the triple to bring in the extra two tricks. To ruff three times in his own hand would ruin his communications. He therefore took the ♡ A and a Heart ruff, entered with a trump for the second ruff, cashed the Spade ace as a Vienna Coup and played trumps to produce:

| | | |
|---|---|---|
| ♠ Q | one-card menace |
| ♡ J | one-card menace |
| ◊ 3 | squeeze card |
| ♣ 2 | communication |

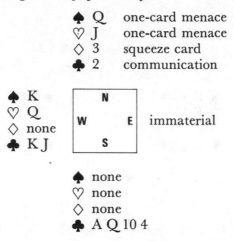

| | | |
|---|---|---|
| ♠ K | | |
| ♡ Q | | |
| ◊ none | | immaterial |
| ♣ K J | | |

| | |
|---|---|
| ♠ none | |
| ♡ none | |
| ◊ none | |
| ♣ A Q 10 4 | |

On the lead of the ◊ 3, the squeeze card, South throwing the
♣ 4, if West throws a Club, South's hand is good; if he throws
either of his other guards, its established menace comes from
North to squeeze him again. Please check what happens if
South trumps three Hearts.

## Criss-cross matrix

| | | |
|---|---|---|
| ♠ 2 | idle card |
| ♡ A | entry |
| ◊ J 2 | long menace |
| ♣ none | |

| | | |
|---|---|---|
| immaterial | | ♠ none |
| | | ♡ K Q |
| | | ◊ K Q |
| | | ♣ none |

| | | |
|---|---|---|
| ♠ 10 | squeeze card |
| ♡ J 2 | long menace |
| ◊ A | entry |
| ♣ none | |

On the play of the squeeze card, the ♠ 10, dummy throws the
idle card (that it follows suit is fortuitous). East must throw one

of his queens. South then cashes *the ace of the suit from which East discarded*, thus establishing the long card of the long menace opposite. He then enters with the other ace to cash that long card. The position is automatic, operative equally well should East's cards be held by West.

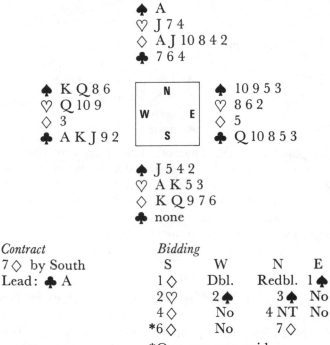

```
                    ♠ A
                    ♡ J 7 4
                    ◇ A J 10 8 4 2
                    ♣ 7 6 4
♠ K Q 8 6                          ♠ 10 9 5 3
♡ Q 10 9        N                  ♡ 8 6 2
◇ 3         W       E              ◇ 5
♣ A K J 9 2         S              ♣ Q 10 8 5 3
                    ♠ J 5 4 2
                    ♡ A K 5 3
                    ◇ K Q 9 7 6
                    ♣ none
```

| *Contract* | *Bidding* | | | |
|---|---|---|---|---|
| 7◇ by South | S | W | N | E |
| Lead: ♣ A | 1◇ | Dbl. | Redbl. | 1♠ |
| | 2♡ | 2♠ | 3♠ | No |
| | 4◇ | No | 4 NT | No |
| | *6◇ | No | 7◇ | |

*One ace, one void

South ruffs the opening lead, enters dummy twice with trumps to ruff two more Clubs and re-enters to play off all dummy's trumps. With one remaining the position is:

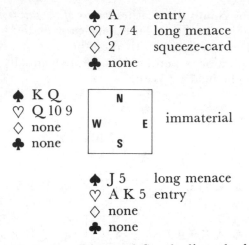

♠ A        entry
♡ J 7 4    long menace
♢ 2        squeeze-card
♣ none

♠ K Q
♡ Q 10 9
♢ none
♣ none

N
W   E    immaterial
S

♠ J 5      long menace
♡ A K 5    entry
♢ none
♣ none

On the play of the last Diamond South discards the ♡ 5. If West throws a Heart, South cashes the A and K, enters with the ♠ A to cash the established ♡ J at Trick 13. If West throws a Spade the ace of that suit is cashed and South's hand becomes high. A fortunate distribution. North, with three Hearts, his partner's second suit, was somewhat optimistic.

**Squeeze before the "count"**

The standard method of attacking the most common types of squeeze is the rectification of the "count", i.e.: the removal of all idle cards from the opponents. This roughly entails losing the maximum number of tricks permissible to the success of the contract and therefore deliberately losing them at an early stage so that the declarer can take control. Once declarer is in control, provided his technique is accurate, there is no defence possible if a genuine position exists. As always, however, there are exceptions to standard practice.

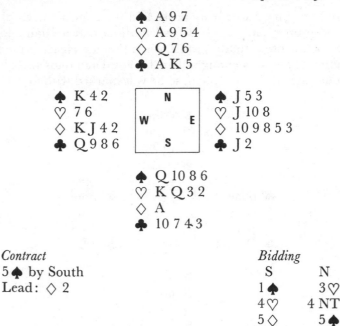

♠ A 9 7
♡ A 9 5 4
◇ Q 7 6
♣ A K 5

♠ K 4 2
♡ 7 6
◇ K J 4 2
♣ Q 9 8 6

♠ J 5 3
♡ J 10 8
◇ 10 9 8 5 3
♣ J 2

♠ Q 10 8 6
♡ K Q 3 2
◇ A
♣ 10 7 4 3

| Contract | Bidding | |
|---|---|---|
| 5 ♠ by South | S | N |
| Lead: ◇ 2 | 1 ♠ | 3 ♡ |
| | 4 ♡ | 4 NT |
| | 5 ◇ | 5 ♠ |
| | No | |

This sequence from one of our leading pairs in a National event has to be recorded in order to be believed. North probably produced the worst sequence of his life. Why he should imagine that South had length in Spades nobody knows. His 4 NT bid asks for aces yet, having discovered that all four were present he still bids only five Spades. Perhaps he needed five aces in order to bid six of something. However, out of the garbage of such auctions sometimes blooms the flower of reasonable dummy-play.

South, taking Trick 1 with his single ace, realised that this hand needed to be played wide open if the contract was to succeed so immediately played ace and another trump, guessing the position correctly. West, winning, returned another trump.

This was information, a guarantee that West held the ◇ K for he would surely have continued the suit otherwise. The hand was now safe provided Clubs also broke evenly but South was taking no chances. He cashed his four tricks in Hearts (which would have been worth six tricks had the contract been played in the proper suit). Both defenders discarded a Diamond but West went into a small huddle when the last Heart came from dummy. That was enough; had he five Diamonds initially he would have had no problem, so he was marked with four Clubs.

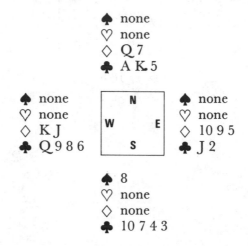

West has yet to play to that last trick so has one card more than the others. If he throws a Diamond, South will ruff dummy's small Diamond, establishing the queen for his eleventh trick. If he throws a Club, ace king and another makes South's hand high. The trick is therefore lost after the squeeze has operated. West is squeezed at Trick 8. If he throws a Club, the trick is lost at Trick 11, if a Diamond at Trick 13.

### Transfer squeeze: transferring the guard

Bridge jargon terms this "Transferring the menace" and the phrase is understood by all players. Actually it should be the guard, not the menace; the menace is with declarer, the guards are with the opponents. And while the menace may also be transferred, this is not essential. In the matrix below both guard and menace are transferred, the ◇ 9 becoming the new menace but the ◇ 3 in the North hand would be equally efficient as a menace and would constitute the main menace were the ◇ 9 and ◇ 3 interchanged.

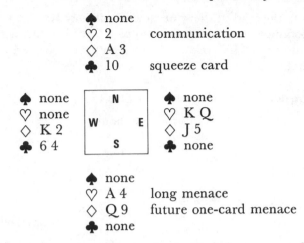

♠ none
♡ 2      communication
♢ A 3
♣ 10     squeeze card

♠ none     [N]     ♠ none
♡ none    [W E]   ♡ K Q
♢ K 2           ♢ J 5
♣ 6 4     [S]     ♣ none

♠ none
♡ A 4     long menace
♢ Q 9     future one-card menace
♣ none

It is impossible to squeeze a player who holds only one guard. That is the situation here, each defender guarding one suit only. So South must arrange for West's guard to be transferred to East, thus making West's hand immaterial and giving East the guards in two suits, thus placing him in a situation where he may be open to squeeze play. The ♢ Q forces West's ♢ K, is taken by dummy's ace, leaving the master with East. The ♣ 10 now forces him either to unguard Hearts or throw that master Diamond, establishing South's ♢ 9.

**Guard squeeze matrix**

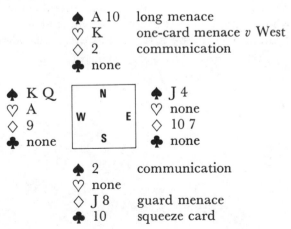

♠ A 10    long menace
♡ K       one-card menace *v* West
♢ 2       communication
♣ none

♠ K Q    [N]     ♠ J 4
♡ A      [W E]   ♡ none
♢ 9            ♢ 10 7
♣ none    [S]     ♣ none

♠ 2       communication
♡ none
♢ J 8     guard menace
♣ 10     squeeze card

On the lead of the squeeze card, the ♣ 10, West cannot afford to unguard either major suit so is forced to throw the ◇ 9. This automatically creates a finesse position against East's Diamond holding.

### Squeeze and throw-in: matrix

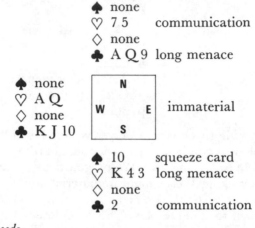

|  |  |  |
|---|---|---|
| ♠ none | | |
| ♡ 7 5 | communication | |
| ◇ none | | |
| ♣ A Q 9 | long menace | |

| ♠ none | | |
| ♡ A Q | | immaterial |
| ◇ none | | |
| ♣ K J 10 | | |

| ♠ 10 | squeeze card |
| ♡ K 4 3 | long menace |
| ◇ none | |
| ♣ 2 | communication |

*South needs*
4 tricks

The play of the ♣ 2 forces West to blank his ♡ A lest dummy take three tricks in Clubs. South throws the ♣ 9, a card no longer working once West has retained his length. He then plays a small Heart to West's ace, establishing his own king to which dummy has communication, and forcing West to lead a Club. The finesse is taken and the ♡ K takes the last trick.

## Simple ruffing squeeze: matrix

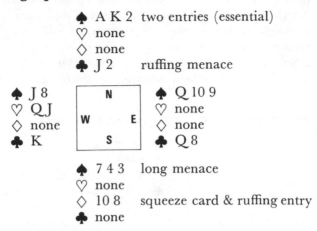

♠ A K 2  two entries (essential)
♡ none
◊ none
♣ J 2    ruffing menace

♠ J 8          ♠ Q 10 9
♡ Q J          ♡ none
◊ none         ◊ none
♣ K            ♣ Q 8

♠ 7 4 3   long menace
♡ none
◊ 10 8    squeeze card & ruffing entry
♣ none

West's hand is not material but is given for convenience. The ◊ 10, the squeeze card, is played, dummy throwing the ♠ 2. If East throws a Club South enters dummy with a top Spade to ruff a small Club, establishing dummy's knave. If he throws a Spade, the two top Spades are cashed, establishing South's third Spade, the entry available via the ruff of a Club.

## Double ruffing squeeze: matrix

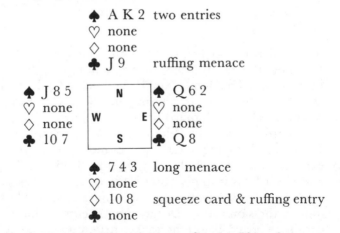

♠ A K 2  two entries
♡ none
◊ none
♣ J 9    ruffing menace

♠ J 8 5        ♠ Q 6 2
♡ none         ♡ none
◊ none         ◊ none
♣ 10 7         ♣ Q 8

♠ 7 4 3   long menace
♡ none
◊ 10 8    squeeze card & ruffing entry
♣ none

On the lead of the ◊ 10 West throws a Spade. If he throws a

Club, dummy is entered with one Spade top and the ♣ J is played, forcing East's queen, pinning West's ten, establishing North's nine. Dummy throws the ♠ 2 and East is in the same situation as was West. If he throws a Club a small one ruffed removes his queen to establish North's knave, so he too throws a Spade. The two top Spades are therefore cashed, establishing South's third card with a trump available as entry.

**Pinning squeeze for no-trumps: matrix**

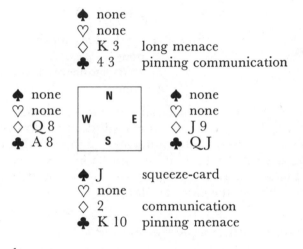

|   |   |   |
|---|---|---|
| ♠ | none | |
| ♡ | none | |
| ◇ | K 3 | long menace |
| ♣ | 4 3 | pinning communication |

|   |   |   |   |   |   |   |
|---|---|---|---|---|---|---|
| ♠ | none | | N | | ♠ | none |
| ♡ | none | W | | E | ♡ | none |
| ◇ | Q 8 | | S | | ◇ | J 9 |
| ♣ | A 8 | | | | ♣ | Q J |

|   |   |   |
|---|---|---|
| ♠ | J | squeeze-card |
| ♡ | none | |
| ◇ | 2 | communication |
| ♣ | K 10 | pinning menace |

*South needs*
3 tricks

The lead of the ♠ J squeezes both defenders. If West throws a Club, South's ♣ 10 drops his ace, establishing South's king, so he throws a Diamond. North discards a Club, still retaining communication to his pinning menace, and East, forced to retain his Diamond guard because his partner has relinquished his guard in the suit, blanks his ♣ Q. South now plays a Diamond, dropping West's queen and so removing his card of exit and then comes dummy's Club, dropping East's queen, and forcing West to give South his ♣ 10 at Trick 13.

In these situations the defenders must each hold two doubletons in the same suits. Declarer must ensure that the last idle card is removed before he makes his pinning play at Trick 12.

## Planning

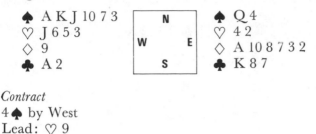

♠ A K J 10 7 3
♡ J 6 5 3
◇ 9
♣ A 2

♠ Q 4
♡ 4 2
◇ A 10 8 7 3 2
♣ K 8 7

*Contract*
4♠ by West
Lead: ♡ 9

South opened the bidding with 1 ♡ but West-East still managed to reach a game in Spades. South takes Trick 1 with the ♡ Q and returns a trump. West, realising that nobody is going to permit him to ruff any of his Hearts, decides to try for an even split in Diamonds. For this he needs entries, so takes Trick 2 in his own hand, leaving the ♠ Q in dummy, and plays the ◇ A and ruffs a Diamond. He exits with a Heart, taken by North's eight, confirming a doubleton, placing South with five. North continues with another trump, following his partner's defence. Dummy wins and West trumps another Diamond. If the suits break evenly, the Diamonds are good, trumps can be drawn and the ♣ K provides the necessary entry. But South fails to follow.

West now makes the key play, discarding his third Heart. Why? He is of course rectifying the count, creating a situation where he has lost the maximum number of tricks permissible, and so has removed the idle cards from the opponents' hands.

North returns a Club but West wins with his ace in hand and is assured of making the contract. Please check. For a squeeze here he needs a long menace against both opponents. He has that with ♣ K 8 in dummy and communication in his own hand. He needs a one-card menace against North. The ◇ 10 is there sitting over North, discarding after him. He needs a one-card menace against South. He has that in the ♡ J, sitting over South and so discarding after him. He simply plays trumps.

The final position will inevitably be:

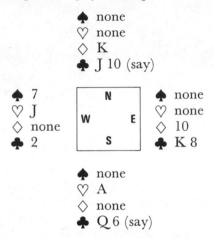

```
            ♠ none
            ♡ none
            ◇ K
            ♣ J 10 (say)

  ♠ 7              N          ♠ none
  ♡ J                         ♡ none
  ◇ none    W          E      ◇ 10
  ♣ 2              S          ♣ K 8

            ♠ none
            ♡ A
            ◇ none
            ♣ Q 6 (say)
```

West leads his last trump. North discards a Club. Dummy now throws the Diamond ten, its work done, and South must either throw his ♡ A, establishing West's knave or making both dummy's Clubs good.

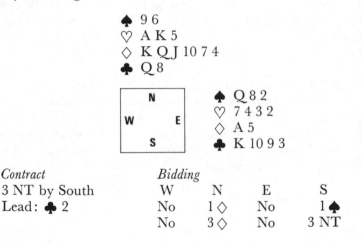

```
            ♠ 9 6
            ♡ A K 5
            ◇ K Q J 10 7 4
            ♣ Q 8

               N          ♠ Q 8 2
                          ♡ 7 4 3 2
          W          E    ◇ A 5
               S          ♣ K 10 9 3
```

| Contract | Bidding | | | |
|---|---|---|---|---|
| 3 NT by South | W | N | E | S |
| Lead: ♣ 2 | No | 1 ◇ | No | 1 ♠ |
| | No | 3 ◇ | No | 3 NT |

East has no serious problem when he sees the lead on which dummy plays low. Three tricks in Clubs can be established quickly and the ◇ A makes four. Partner's lead is low from a picture, ace or knave. East's normal play is therefore the ♣ 9 which, if South has the knave, clears the suit, if the ace, is good enough to force it without establishing dummy's queen.

But of course South does not have the ace. Please check. East therefore plays the king and switches to the ♠ 8. This, to his partner looks like top of nothing and anyway, after the bidding, cannot be an attempt to establish a Spade suit. It is therefore an attempt to take one trick in Spades before going back to Clubs. South with ♠ A J 10 6, cannot afford to take the trick for that leaves him with two losers each in Spades and Clubs plus the ◇ A. So perforce he ducks. West wins and clears the Clubs and South now loses one Spade, one Diamond and three Clubs.

South is of course marked with the ♣ J on his play of a small card from dummy. If he had the ace he would have played the queen. East's possession of the ♣ 10 is the key to this knowledge. Q 2 opposite A 4 3 must play the queen. Q 2 opposite J 4 3 must play small.

Should East lack that ten the situation is entirely different. Q 2 opposite A 10 4 must play small to guarantee two tricks in the suit. Q 2 opposite J 10 4 can play any card without any effect. The situations are important. In the hand above, the contract is absolutely safe if the Clubs are cleared before that Spade trick is secured. The vital tempo has been lost.

|  |  |  |
|---|---|---|
| ♠ J 9 6 5 | | ♠ A Q 4 2 |
| ♡ K 4 2 | N | ♡ A Q J 6 |
| ◇ K 7 | W    E | ◇ A Q J |
| ♣ A 7 3 2 | S | ♣ K 4 |

*Contract*
6 NT by West
Lead : ♡ 8

The play is straightforward, is it not? We take the first lead in hand and then finesse the ♠ Q. South shows void. We have of course played incorrectly and been fortunate in that it has cost us nothing. The Spades should have been played ace first to guard against a singleton king with South. If South follows, the next lead of the suit is the queen, in case South holds K 10 to four when the position will be exposed and the finesse of the nine will be available.

But what now? Well, North had initially five cards in Spades so eight others. We can actually play off nine tops outside

Spades so, unless he is two-suited, we may well be able to strip him of his outside cards and produce some sort of end-play. North follows to three Hearts and to three Diamonds so the hand is now over; unless he has a fourth Diamond.

| ♠ J 9 6 | | ♠ A 4 2 |
| ♡ none | N | ♡ none |
| ◇ none | W   E | ◇ none |
| ♣ A 7 | S | ♣ K 4 |

The two Clubs are cashed, North following to the first, discarding a Spade on the second, but he discarded a Club on the fourth Heart so all is well.

```
              ♠ K 10 8
             ┌─────────┐
             │    N    │
   ♠ J 9 6   │ W     E │   ♠ A 4 2
             │    S    │
             └─────────┘
```

A small Spade goes to the knave. Note that the position is unchanged if East has the ♠ Q now instead of the ♠ A.

```
 ♠ A K J 10 9   ┌─────────┐   ♠ Q 4 2
 ♡ K Q 10 3 2   │    N    │   ♡ A 5
 ◇ A 9          │ W     E │   ◇ J 3 2
 ♣ 5            │    S    │   ♣ A 10 8 6 4
                └─────────┘
```

*Contract*
7♠ by West
Lead: ♣ K

*Bidding*

| W | E |
|---|---|
| 2♣ | 3♣ |
| 3♠ | 4♠ |
| 4 NT | 5♡ (two aces) |
| 7♠ | |

Ambitious? Probably, the expectation of four cards in Spades being disappointed. Please make your plan.

The opening lead has killed any hope for a squeeze. On another lead, say a trump (quite normal against grand slams), we could hope for a break in Hearts, the ◇ A cashed as a Vienna Coup and the defender holding ♣ K Q J and ◇ K

Q 10 would be squeezed. Far-fetched indeed. (Our last two cards would be ◇ 9 and ♣ 5, dummy's ♣ A 10 and the defenders would have to discard from three.) But reality! Somehow we have to get rid of those two losing Diamonds in dummy and it must be on Hearts. And there must be a trump remaining in dummy so that we can ruff our own losing Diamond. We can draw two rounds of trumps only therefore. If the Hearts break the plan fails for no matter which defender has the long trump he will play it on the fourth Heart. So the Hearts must be four-two and the defender with the four has three trumps.

Now how do we play the Hearts? Bang out the tops and hope that the knave drops doubleton? Odds are 2–1 against that; the knave should be with the four. So: ♣ A, draw two rounds of trumps; ♡ A finesse ♡ 10; cash two more Hearts, discarding dummy's Diamonds; ◇ A, ruff Diamond, back to hand ruffing a Club; draw last trump and claim. Simple. But then all dummy-plays are simple once they have been successful.

 ♠ A 2     ♠ K Q 7 4
 ♡ 10 5 3    ♡ A K 4
 ◇ A 9 6 4 3   ◇ K 7 5
 ♣ J 6 2     ♣ A K 8

*Contract*
6 ◇ by West
Lead: ♡ 6

All we need do here is make our plan. Please do so while I take time out to make mine.

All right, my first plan is made: take ♡ A and duck a round of trumps. Take second Heart and draw trumps. Cash ♣ A and K as double Vienna Coup to leave ♣ J as menace against ♣ Q. Return to hand with ♠ A to produce:

| communication | ♠ 2 | | ♠ K Q 7 | long menace |
| one-card menace | ♡ 10 | | ♡ none | |
| squeeze card | ◇ 9 | | ◇ none | |
| one-card menace | ♣ J | | ♣ 8 | idle card |

Not bad. We have here a standard four-card ending for a double automatic simultaneous. On the lead of the ♢ 9 North must keep his master Heart so has to throw a Spade if that is his idle card. Dummy throws the Club and now South, guarding Spades and with the ♣ Q is helpless. Very neat. The danger, however, is that one defender may hold both one-card guards while the other has a hand consisting of Spades and nothing else.

Is there a better way? Of course the fall of cards may assist us to assess the actual situation but we haven't had any fall up to now. We are still wondering what to play to Trick 2. We could of course cash both top Hearts, both top trumps, all three top Spades, discarding our third Heart, ruff dummy's Heart loser, play a Club to the ace and return the fourth Spade, ruffing that to produce:

|  |  |  |  |
|---|---|---|---|
| ♠ none | | N | ♠ none |
| ♡ none | W | E | ♡ none |
| ♢ 9 | | | ♢ 7 |
| ♣ J 6 | | S | ♣ K 8 |

If the Spade is not over-ruffed we play the last trump and hope that the defender who wins it has queen and another Club left. If it is over-ruffed that defender will have to return a Club or concede a ruff-and-discard. So basically we have played the hand on the simple assumption that the player with the three trumps also holds the ♣ Q.

In our first effort we played it on the assumption that the player who held the four Spades also held the ♣ Q, *or* also held the master Heart. This seems to be a better chance and the decision is reinforced when we consider that for one player to have precisely three trumps is a necessity, whereas there is no necessity for a player to have four Spades. He could have five, ruff the third round and exit with his master Heart, we not having had time yet to ruff that third Heart in dummy. The contract would depend upon the ♣ Q falling doubleton.

|  |  |  |  |
|---|---|---|---|
| ♠ A Q J | | N | ♠ K 10 4 2 |
| ♡ A Q 9 6 | W | E | ♡ K J 5 |
| ♢ K 8 3 | | | ♢ A 9 5 2 |
| ♣ K 9 2 | | S | ♣ Q 7 |

*Contract*
6 NT by West
Lead: ♠ 7

How do we plan this one? Basically it's easy enough—as long as Diamonds are reasonably divided and so are Clubs and we can find the ♣ A on the left and the ♣ J 10 on the right, all is well. Or perhaps four Diamonds and the ♣ A on the left; that would do. Of course we can also make it if the ♣ A is on the right, provided it is bolstered by the ♣ J 10 or, alternatively five small cards, either way plus four cards in Diamonds. Or any such hand with extra length in the minors. After that one might think it difficult to go down. Let's see how it goes. Obviously we must try the Club first.

We lead small to the ♣ Q and it wins. Now we must hope for one of our suitable positions and come down to a pinning menace in Clubs, a long, split menace in Diamonds and a squeeze card. Easy enough to produce the position with our own cards.

| ♠ | none | |
|---|---|---|
| ♡ | Q | squeeze card |
| ◇ | K 8 | short end of long, split menace |
| ♣ | K 9 | pinning menace |

♣ A on left, ♣ J 10 on right, Diamonds fairly split and there we are.

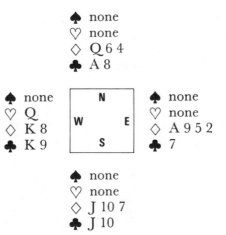

|  | ♠ none |  |
|---|---|---|
|  | ♡ none |  |
|  | ◇ Q 6 4 |  |
|  | ♣ A 8 |  |

| ♠ none | | ♠ none |
|---|---|---|
| ♡ Q | N | ♡ none |
| ◇ K 8 | W      E | ◇ A 9 5 2 |
| ♣ K 9 | S | ♣ 7 |

|  | ♠ none |
|---|---|
|  | ♡ none |
|  | ◇ J 10 7 |
|  | ♣ J 10 |

On the lead of the ♡ Q North throws a Diamond lest we play a small Club to his singleton ace and so establish our twelfth trick. Dummy throws a Diamond. South cannot throw a Diamond or else dummy's third Diamond will be good, so he throws the ♣ 10. We may now either play the ♣ K, forcing the ace, pinning the knave and so establishing our extra trick, or play two rounds of Diamonds, ending in dummy and play the Club from there, North winning Trick 12 but being forced to lead his ♣ 8 to our ♣ 9 as Trick 13. If we do play like that we must of course play both Diamonds, not merely one, for that latter would leave North with a card of exit.

If North had held ♣ A J 10 or ♣ A to any six cards plus four cards in Diamonds (or ◇ Q J 10 alone) the end-position would have been:

♠ none
♡ none
◇ Q J 10
♣ A J

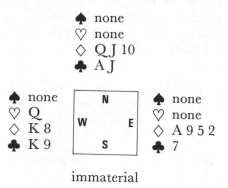

♠ none       ♠ none
♡ Q         ♡ none
◇ K 8       ◇ A 9 5 2
♣ K 9       ♣ 7

immaterial

and he would again have been helpless when we lead the ♡ Q. If South had held those cards:

immaterial

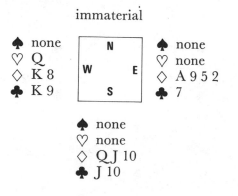

♠ none       ♠ none
♡ Q         ♡ none
◇ K 8       ◇ A 9 5 2
♣ K 9       ♣ 7

♠ none
♡ none
◇ Q J 10
♣ J 10

and, having lost the ♣ A at Trick 1 the lead of the ♡ Q would bring in all the tricks. South's return on winning that ace does not affect this in any way except pictorially. The hands would contain a Diamond or a Club fewer, a four-card instead of a five-card position but just as effective. A solid study should perhaps be made here, laying out the cards for each position.

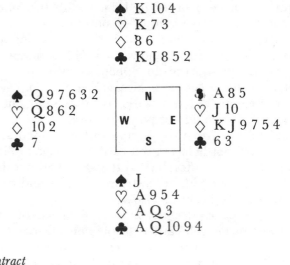

♠ K 10 4
♡ K 7 3
◇ 8 6
♣ K J 8 5 2

♠ Q 9 7 6 3 2
♡ Q 8 6 2
◇ 10 2
♣ 7

♠ A 8 5
♡ J 10
◇ K J 9 7 5 4
♣ 6 3

♠ J
♡ A 9 5 4
◇ A Q 3
♣ A Q 10 9 4

*Contract*
6♣ by South
Lead: ♠ 6

One of the world's outstanding dummy-players failed to make this hand, yet the play was well within his capability. Clearly Homer nodded. As a coda, therefore, we will analyse the harmonic progression, following the sequence of thought which here leads inexorably to the right play.

The contract is of course terrible and that ranking players reach such contracts provides a modicum of reassurance to lesser mortals. The odds against success are something over 60–1. We need the Spade finesse and the Diamond finesse, the Hearts to break 4–2 with the four in one particular hand and we must have a Spade lead. (This last with a rare exception, i.e.: West holding every Spade higher than the ♠ 4, except East's ace. This is because in the final situation, dummy's ♠ 4 is our one-card menace and if East can guard against it West may discard his entire holding and so avoid being squeezed.) 60–1 against therefore, yet, as we progress, these odds diminish with extraordinary speed. The actual play is small from dummy at Trick 1 to East's ace, a Diamond switch enforcing a winning finesse and three of our necessities have already been supplied. The odds against us are now roughly a mere 3–1. All that we now require is the 4–2 break in Hearts with the four in the suitable hand, i.e.: 50 per cent of 48 per cent.

Declarer drew trumps, cashed the ♠ K, throwing a Heart, ruffed dummy's third Spade and rattled off his trumps. Clearly he was playing to squeeze an opponent over the red suits, hoping that the hand with four Hearts held also six Diamonds. As we can see, this did not work. What is more, he should have known that it could not possibly work.

East had followed to two trumps and two Spades. Consequently he could not hold ten red cards. West had followed to one trump and two Spades, but, as the ♠ Q had not dropped, he must have started with at least three Spades and that ruled ten red cards out of his hand also.

Once that happened declarer must look elsewhere. On comparison of evidence, even earlier, to play on Diamonds is bad; we have no guarantee of any sort of length—merely a hope, and this, up against the certainty we have of the position of the ♠ Q, should clearly lead us to retain that ♠ 10 in dummy as our one-card menace, nicely placed positionally.

It is clear that, in order to obtain an extra trick, we must ruff something, either a Spade in hand or a Diamond in dummy. Once the ruff of the Spade is ruled out by the impossibility of our third Diamond being a genuine menace, the Diamond ruff must be taken.

West shows out on the third round. So East started with six. Having shown four black cards he might have three Hearts but cannot possibly have four. Immediately the odds against this contract being made improve again. If Hearts break 4–2 the only hand which can hold the four is West and, as the break is a 48 per cent chance, so is now our contract. Instead of being 60-odd to 1 against, it is now almost even money.

Two more rounds of trumps therefore bring us to our position.

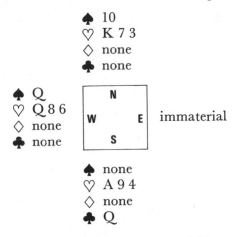

♠ 10
♡ K 7 3
◇ none
♣ none

♠ Q
♡ Q 8 6
◇ none
♣ none

immaterial

♠ none
♡ A 9 4
◇ none
♣ Q

The lead of the ♣ Q forces West to unguard Hearts in order to preserve his master Spade and our long menace in Hearts is now established. In practice there might be no need to play the hand through. Should East discard a Spade on a trump we may table our cards and claim, for with six Diamonds and now five black cards he cannot hold more than two Hearts.

In the published analysis of this hand the (quite famous) analyst stated that the hand "was a make after all" and produced a five-card ending instead of our four-carder, having retained the ♠ K. This, I fear, is double-dummy analysis, not available in actual play.

If that ♠ K is not cashed we cannot discover the exact shape of the defenders' hands. The doubleton ♠ K 10 looks like a long menace but without communication it is useless as such and should be reduced to a one-card menace. Retention of unnecessary length flouts one of the first rules of squeeze-play—the removal of idle cards from the defenders.

Sometimes we do "squeeze without the count" but that little piece of bridge jargon can be misleading; it does not mean that we lack the hand-count, but have not "rectified" the trick-count. The hand-count remains important even with that type of squeeze. Here we obtain it by cashing that ♠ K, and only then is the play of the hand technically acceptable.

*Notes*

*Notes*

*Notes*

*Notes*